Take Your Invention to Market

Dale Davis

Self-Counsel Press
(a subsidiary of)
International Self-Counsel Press Ltd.
USA   Canada

Library and Archives Canada Cataloguing in Publication

Davis, Dale A. (Dale Allen)
    Take your invention to market / Dale Davis.

(Self-counsel business series)
ISBN 1-55180-597-9

1. New products--Marketing. I. Title. II. Series.
HF5415.153.D384 2005   658.5'75   C2004-906707-9

Self-Counsel Press
(a subsidiary of)
International Self-Counsel Press Ltd.

1704 N. State Street	1481 Charlotte Road
Bellingham, WA 98225	North Vancouver, BC V7J 1H1
USA	Canada

CONTENTS

Notice to Readers

Preface

This book has come into your life because you have an idea, a product, or an invention you want to take to market. Keep reading and you'll learn everything you need to know to do just that.

I love marketing and understanding why one product sells while another sits on the shelf. I want to fully understand people's perception of a product and what makes one product more appealing than another. I see marketing as a problem to be solved for industry and a solution to be provided for the consumer. Marketing is fundamentally identifying a need and filling it.

My education in marketing started when I was a young boy in the seventh grade, living near Los Angeles. I discovered that the candy from the vending machine across the street from the school tasted unusually good. The problem was that if we got caught sneaking across the street to snag some, we risked being expelled from school. When my friends found out I was taking this chance, they asked me to get some for them too.

That's when I learned about the concept of "value added," a marketing term that simply means something of value is added to the product. This "something" is often what sets one product

A dream, by itself, is not enough. You need to add a good dose of practicality to the formula if you hope to market your idea successfully.

apart from another. In this case, the candy from the vending machine had an added value of risk, which upped the price I could resell it for to my friends. I had inadvertently uncovered a business opportunity. A dime could make me twenty cents, doubling my money. I found this prospect even more exciting than sneaking across the street. Before I knew it, I was taking orders and selling candy on a daily basis.

It's funny to think back and realize that Sweet Tarts and Sour Apple Gum taught me my first lessons about marketing. I was solving problems for my customers, who didn't want to risk getting caught, but who wanted the vending machine candy enough to pay me extra for it.

Soon afterwards, I began to learn the lessons of supply and demand. My supply from the vending machine was not keeping up with the demand, so I had to find another supply source. I quickly got myself organized, came up with another strategy, and before I knew it had my first small business to run.

I found that I could buy candy from the store even cheaper than from the vending machine if I bought larger quantities. I would load up my pockets with candy and gum in the morning and come home at night with a pocketful of change. The candy didn't even have to come from the vending machine; the kids bought it anyway. I also discovered that the convenience of my being on the school grounds added value.

I didn't realize it at the time, but I was diverting funds from other markets. The money that my schoolmates received from their parents to buy a healthy lunch was instead coming to me.

That was 1969. I was 14 and becoming known as the "candyman." Some classmates were even putting in standing orders. I was cruising along on my success. Then suddenly it all came to a screeching halt when my parents announced we were moving to Oklahoma. Life as I knew it was over.

I will never forget my feeling of doom at the prospect of being transplanted in the mid-west. Oklahoma was definitely not a cool place to be. I considered myself a hippie and a child of the sixties. I wore bell-bottom pants, a guru shirt, and beads. I even had boots with leather tassels.

To add insult to injury, my parents moved to a small town called Owasso, about 20 miles north of Tulsa. I was stuck in a hick town that didn't even have a streetlight! This wasn't going to be any fun.

Fortunately, my newly acquired marketing skills came to the rescue in my struggle to adapt. Standing out as I did in a small community meant that selling candy to my fellow students was out of the question. I had to find something that worked for a different crowd — one that I clearly didn't relate to.

I figured that if my marketing savvy had served me well in California, it could serve me just as well in Oklahoma. I had a sense of being more street-wise than my classmates. But selling something that positioned me as smarter than others didn't have a lot of marketing appeal to say the least. It was going to be a challenge, but I was going to try to market my difference, maybe even my knowledge.

I first tested the waters in my drafting class. For me, drafting was an easy A if I just showed up and did the work. The teacher even let me take the work home if I didn't get it done in class. This situation presented my first business opportunity: to sell completed homework assignments to my lazier, less ambitious classmates. I would finish my drawing assignment and then make copies to sell before class. At first I charged $1 a sheet, but by the end of the year I was getting $10. This success gave me the idea to sell homework assignments in other classes. Later I added selling school supplies to my list of services. I sold T-squares and triangles I made from scrap Plexiglas. I sold lead pencils. I even built a light table to improve production for the drafting homework assignments.

But then the inevitable happened — the teacher caught on to me. One day he noticed that the class assignments all looked pretty much alike. Comparing the writing revealed that the lettering was the same. It didn't take him long to identify the culprit.

Before I could conjure up excuses as to why the homework assignments looked similar, I decided to come clean. To my surprise he was so impressed with my ingenuity that he said he would let it go if I promised not to do it anymore.

A couple of weeks later I even sold him a paddle made out of scrap Plexiglas, which he promised he wouldn't use on me since I had given him my word about going straight. Then, when he showed it off to the other teachers, I got two more orders! Marketing had put me ahead of the game once again.

Without realizing it at the time, I learned about marketing in other classes as well. For example, in band class, we were always being asked to raise money for one event or another by selling candy or raffle tickets door-to-door. This experience turned out to be the start of my own door-to-door selling of other products. I figured if I could sell for the school, I could sell for myself.

My first adventure was selling pantyhose. When this didn't work out to my liking, I switched to selling office and printing supplies to businesses, which proved more successful.

My next lessons in marketing came during my first job at a car lot, where I learned that persistence really does pay off. Without a car of my own, I decided to get a job at the only business within walking distance from my home, a Chevrolet dealership across the highway. I asked about openings and was told there were none.

Undaunted, I went back the next day. Same question, same answer. I went back again the next day and the next. Within a week they had created a job for me. I started out as a car duster. I kept the cars in the showroom dust free, and I did an excellent job of it. I soon got promoted to the detail shop where I washed and detailed used cars.

Before long, I had earned enough money to buy my own car. It wasn't the car I had envisioned, but nonetheless it was a car. A pink Rambler — at least until I sprayed it with 20 cans of candy apple blue paint. That was some paint job! My whole family got involved. Since I could not afford chrome wheels, I made my own by gluing kitchen foil to the wheels.

Once I had a car, I soon figured out how to make more money. I used the only work skills I had and started a detail business in the evening for the only other car lot in town. After I got off work at the first lot, I would pick up a car at the other lot and drive it home to detail. I charged $25 per car — big money in 1972!

That experience also taught me about marketing risk. One night while dropping off a car at the lot, I got a little more than I had bargained for. When I turned around after locking the car door, I came face-to-face with a police officer pointing a gun at me. I'm not sure who jumped higher, but the one thing I do remember was that his gun was shaking. He was more scared than I was.

I explained that I was not stealing the car or taking it for a joyride, but he took me to the police station anyway. Fortunately, my boss was contacted and I was cleared. After that experience, I gave some thought to risk management.

I can't remember not having some kind of business going. I've marketed art, photography, tomato plants, pen stripping, signs, business services, technical and creative writing, silk screening, and more. I remember selling an $800 order for silk screening before even learning how to silk screen! I figured, how hard can it be? Sometimes the only secret to success is just doing it. The people who take risks and "just do it" are entrepreneurs.

It was that kind of thinking that led me to become a full-time product developer and inventor. I have invented and licensed my own products internationally. I have also produced and sold unpatented products that I delivered myself to local stores, which taught me about the supply side of the business.

The inventor or creative entrepreneur is a unique kind of person who sees opportunity where others see problems.

I wish I could say that all of my ideas have been successful. Some have worked better than others, but all of them have taught me well, even if sometimes it was what not to do next time. I've also been lucky to have worked for some large corporations such as StairMaster, Zebco, and Lowrance Electronics. I developed new products, patented new ideas, or worked in research and development for these companies.

Working many years as a product designer and a patent consultant has allowed me to learn from some of the brightest and most experienced innovators around. I've also worked with some people whose ideas cost them everything they owned. I've seen successes that made me scratch my head. And I've seen failures that had nothing to do with the product and everything to do with the marketing.

The inventor or creative entrepreneur is a unique kind of person who sees opportunity where others see problems. Entrepreneurs love to solve problems. They understand that necessity is many times the driving force behind new business. The typical entrepreneur thrives on the excitement of developing new business ventures.

Some entrepreneurs started out by trying to be an entrepreneur. Others I call "accidental entrepreneurs" because they never intended on being in their own business. These people somehow find themselves in business because they are out of work, need extra money, or see a problem needing a solution. Many of these businesses are part-time and are becoming an important part of our economy.

Some people are "weekend entrepreneurs," a category I've occupied myself at times. While working at full-time positions, I've written and published several books. I've also received development money and grants from the Department of Defense and Department of Energy on projects started out of my home. I've invented and internationally licensed products that began in my garage.

Whether your status is as a weekend, accidental, or full-time entrepreneur, never underestimate the power of starting small. I've told many of my customers to let the product earn its own way. I've seen too many people get hung up on the process and forget about the end results — spending so much on protecting their idea that few resources are left to promote it.

I can't remember all the people who have told me that someone else took their idea and made the money while they were holding on tight and waiting for the world to discover them. Marketing your ideas and yourself aggressively is the only way I know to get discovered.

The lessons in this book are from the many inventors I've worked with as well as my own. This book will tell you what tools you need, but it can't pick them up and use them for you. This book will give you knowledge, but it can't make you use it. It's going to be your strength and sheer will power that will move you toward success. Remember, it's not always what you know, but what you do with what you know that counts. So believe in your success, stay focused, and market well!

Introduction

Some of us look at life a bit differently than most. And, because you are reading this book, I suspect you are one of these people. Perhaps you are an inventor or an entrepreneur, or you are otherwise very creative. You likely have some kind of dream — of an idea, a product, a business, and you're driven by a desire to turn that dream into reality. As a dreamer, you share a special kinship with all dreamers of the past, present, and future.

Thomas Edison was a dreamer. He dreamed of a longer-lasting lamp that could be operated by electricity. He believed in his innovation, and despite many failures, the ambition that arose from his desire helped turn his dream into reality.

While almost everyone is born with that special capacity to dream — to look at the world full of wonder and curiosity — most of us lose that capacity as we grow older, taking the world with all its wonders for granted. But for the inventor or entrepreneur starting a new business or developing an idea, some of that wonder remains. Much of modern industry was created and developed by entrepreneurs who started with a simple idea. These dreamers have been responsible for much of the country's gross national product and many of the new jobs created in the private sector.

These same entrepreneurs have produced many more innovations than all the large corporations combined.

Yet for every success, there are hundreds of failures that we never hear about. Failure is not a topic many like to talk about. You aren't likely to want to buy a book about all the ideas that didn't get to market — despite the fact that most successes result from earlier failures. But failure is also part of the creative process — part of the path to successful marketing. Like a child learning to walk, you may have to take a few tumbles along the way before you can walk upright without support.

By reading this book, I hope that you feel that there is someone behind you all the way, ready to catch you when you fall, ready to keep you headed in the right direction in your path to marketing your idea. You'll soon discover that there are many steps along the way, and that your idea or concept will be tested time and time again.

A dream, by itself, is not enough. You need to add a good dose of practicality to the formula if you hope to market your idea successfully. This book provides that practical information. It covers:

- Evaluating your idea (chapter 1)
- Protecting yourself legally (chapter 2)
- What and how to research (chapter 3)
- Why you need a prototype and how to make one (chapter 4)
- How to market your product or idea (chapter 5)
- Financial considerations (chapter 6)
- Licensing (chapter 7)

Also included is a useful appendix of contacts that will jumpstart your plan for earning your market share.

This book gives you the tools to turn that dream of yours into reality. Your chances of success will depend on your determination and willingness to learn, adapt, and work hard. Your reward is the satisfaction that comes with success and seeing your idea become real. And with the right formula of research, timing, and a bit of luck, financial rewards will soon follow.

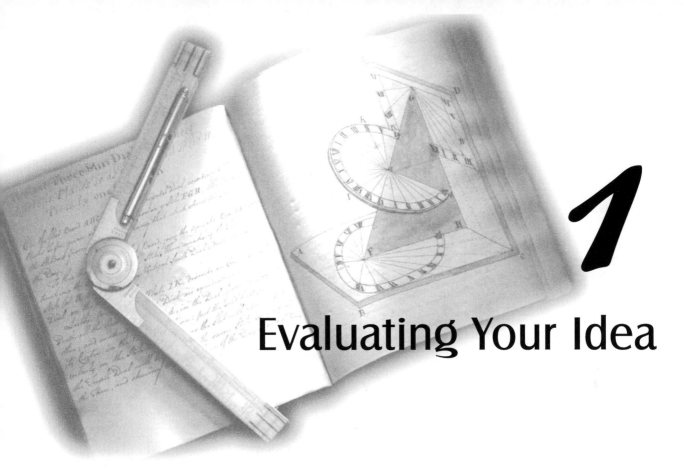

Evaluating Your Idea

Many modern inventions were dreamed of centuries ago by Leonardo da Vinci (1452–1519), the Italian Renaissance artist, architect, and engineer. Leonardo's idea for a helicopter, for example, was later developed by Enrico Forlani in 1878. It flew for only 20 seconds, but it was the forerunner of the modern helicopter, which became a reality in 1936.

1. Learning to Be Your Own Devil's Advocate

So you have an idea. It's a good idea, of course, or you wouldn't be thinking about how to get it to market. You wouldn't have the faith that thousands, like you, are waiting to get their hands on that idea — whether it be a product, an invention, or some other "great new thing."

But the truth is, there are no perfect ideas. There are a lot of bad ideas that have somehow made it to the market. Some products

A lot if good ideas fail to get to market because of lack of financing.

have so much money behind them that they are forced upon us in such a way that eventually we accept them. There are also a lot of good ideas and products still sitting in someone's closet because they never got the financing to get them to the market.

How do you know whether your idea is viable? How do you know that your enthusiasm will be shared by others?

First, you need to do some hard self-assessment, by being your own devil's advocate. If you don't take on this role of carefully critiquing your idea, which means assessing it from many different angles, sooner or later someone else will. And that can set you back in time, money, and energy.

You need to anticipate what questions the market will have. The sooner you know how to respond to the naysayers, the more likely you will succeed. You can't afford to take your idea to market if it is full of weaknesses. If you do, it won't be long before someone starts improving upon those weaknesses and steals your market share.

I learned this lesson early on with my first invention, the Fire Guardian, a heat-activated fire extinguisher for use in homes. I knew back then that thousands of people were dying each year in their own homes because of a lack of fire protection. I had also patented a new way to produce this invention that would allow for the product to retail for about $25, not the $300 that the nearest competitor was charging.

I can still remember presenting my idea at one of my first inventors' association meetings over 20 years ago. One man raked me over the coals and did his best to humiliate me in front of the whole group. In his opinion, I was wasting my time and money and nobody was ever going to buy my idea anyway. I found myself getting so flustered by his comments that my presentation fell apart. I was shocked to find out that someone did not support my idea — an idea that saved lives no less — and I took the criticism very personally.

But that experience helped me in two ways. First, I came to understand that I needed to separate myself from my invention. In this case, the man was criticizing the invention, not me. And second, I learned that criticism was extremely helpful. As I continued in my quest to market the Fire Guardian, I found that his negative comments only strengthened my resolve to become a success.

Later, after looking more closely at my product, I discovered that he had brought up some points I needed to consider. The product at that time was too large, so I thought about how to make it smaller. I then thought about other markets I could approach with a smaller unit. I wanted to have the best product possible, but also realized that even a less-than-perfect product would solve the market need.

2. Defining Your Idea: Put It in Writing

The first step to clearly defining your idea, and to being able to assess it thoroughly, is to put it in writing. To make it real, write it down. Write why you feel your creation is better, improved, or different than existing products. This exercise will help you identify any weaknesses you may have to address, or questions you still have to answer.

Defining your idea in this way serves more than one purpose. I've found that most inventors and creative thinkers have a tendency to let others worry about the details, even when those details are the obstacles. These obstacles may keep the idea from the market if not considered up-front. Another purpose for defining your idea lies in the knowledge you will gain by having to understand a process well enough to explain it.

You can get started by asking yourself, and writing answers to, the following questions:

- What is your idea? What does it do?

- Why is your idea so different?

- Who will use your invention?

2.1 What is your idea? What does it do?

You first need to clearly define what your invention or idea is, and what it does. Describe it. Name it. Explain why other products and means do not work as well. Why should someone use your product and not someone else's? What are the advantages of using your product? How does your product really stand up to the competition?

Be as specific and detailed as possible. Take a look at the competition and try writing down a description of what that product does. Compare and evaluate with an open mind. Many times this process can help you to further develop your own product. You can start a wish list: If your product could be designed to be absolutely perfect, what would it do? From there, you might just be able to create that perfect product.

2.2 Why is your idea so different?

When answering this question, you need to think like someone who is selling your product to the end user. For example, if your product is made of plastic and the competitor's is made of steel, you need to explain why plastic is being used and why it is better. You also need to know the price of the material you are considering and its properties.

This detailed comparison will help you discover if you need to do more research on the construction of your product. For example, if your product is made of plastic, have you compared polyethylene to polypropylene? Can you explain the advantages and disadvantages of different constructions? If you need more details to help you define the differences of your product, you can do research on the Internet or at the library.

Each of these questions is important to your success, and each is expanded on in the remaining chapters of this book. Once you've read through the remaining chapters, you'll want to come back to this exercise and add to your written description.

2.3 Who will use your invention?

It's also very important to list your potential customers. You must understand who your target market is. It's not enough to simply state that everyone will want and use the product.

In order to establish a target market list, you need to first determine what makes a potential customer. Will your product be for a certain age group? Will it solve a particular problem? Will it be purchased only once or will it be purchased multiple times?

For example, if you have an idea for a product for new mothers, you can research the number of babies born each year and start determining a potential number of customers. You can further break this down into demographics and economic divisions within certain geographical areas to determine where your target markets are located.

Understanding where your market is will further help you understand how to reach that market. It will also show you where to best do test marketing and where to best spend your marketing dollars. Determining where and how to reach these markets will also help you develop a business plan, which is necessary when you want to find investors.

Even if you do not intend to do any of the marketing yourself, this information will be required to get others interested. The more knowledge you have, the better chance you have of convincing others that you understand your product. Knowledge is power. It can also help you determine what an idea is worth when it comes to licensing.

2.4 Making your wish list

One approach for putting all the steps together is to develop a "wish list" for your new product. It might include these topics:

- Type of construction
- Size
- Construction materials
- Features
- Appearance, such as color or texture
- Packaging considerations
- Any bells and whistles

Next, break this list down. For example, you might decide that you want steel construction because it can be machined or formed. That may be an expensive way to produce the product, but plastic tooling can cost hundreds of thousands of dollars. Making this kind of practical costing decision can sometimes be more important to your chances of success than developing the perfect product.

Similarly, the size of a product may be smaller or larger than you would ultimately want. But getting the product out in front of the public, no matter what size, can start the cash flow coming in. Remember, the second version of the product, which you can work on once you have tested the first, will always be better.

My first fire protection product sold for $75. It cost me $25 to produce, and the $50 in profits went back into research and development. This helped me raise money to further develop the product, one that was later produced with plastic nylon material and had many more features than the original.

3. Assessing Your Idea

Now that you've defined your idea in writing, you need to objectively evaluate it. This may be one of the most difficult tasks you face, because you risk being told that your idea, which you have become so attached to, isn't appealing to others.

As mentioned earlier, you first need to assess your idea yourself. But eventually you need to call on others to test whether it is viable. This doesn't mean getting friends to assist, however, because even a true friend won't necessarily tell you that your idea stinks or won't work. When it comes to the real market, there are no friends to buy your product. If it's a bad idea, you need to know now, while corrections can still be made.

Evaluating your idea will ensure that you spend your energy in the right place at the right time. You may discover that you have a great idea, but its time hasn't yet come. Or perhaps it has already passed. Many creative people in the past came up with ideas that were ahead of their time. Some products can take years to take hold while others literally become an overnight success.

For example, would a pet rock sell today like it did 20 years ago? Would today's youth give up a Game Cube for a Frisbee? Evaluating timing is just as important as evaluating the product or idea. I have licensed several products in my career that I know would not stand a chance today.

The two best ways of getting objective feedback on your idea are to poll a group of strangers and to join an inventors' association.

3.1 Test the water: Ask 20 strangers

In this case, unlike most situations, strangers are better than friends. Strangers will be honest. If they don't like it, they will most likely tell you. Others will tell you that they like your product, but they wouldn't buy it. The marketplace you need to be successful in is full of strangers, and you can use their opinions to improve on your product or idea, or to take a different turn.

You may be asking yourself how you are going to find 20 strangers and how to make sure they represent a variety of opinions.

Depending on the product, you will most likely know where your target market lies. For example, if it's industrial, you may have to phone companies and ask if someone could use your product on a test basis. If you want to market a consumer product, there may be stores that can help you. If, for example, you are selling a baby product, you can approach a store specializing in baby products and ask the manager if you can interview customers in the store.

Store managers love to make their customers feel special. Many managers will set up a table for you and some will even promote your idea in advertisements to attract more people to their store.

Look for other opportunities too. Anywhere you can set up a booth, such as a trade show, is a great place to evaluate your product. If you're not shy, you can even stop people on the street and ask them for a few minutes to assess your idea.

You don't have to have a product in hand to start testing the water. While it is helpful to have a sample to show people, you can still get valuable feedback early in the game by simply describing your product or idea. Once you do have a sample in hand, you can carry out the evaluation again. (It's a good idea to keep contact information on the people you interview, so you can follow up with later test marketing — see chapter 5 on marketing.)

Once you have established your test market group, you'll want to ask them a set of standard questions. You will need to vary the questions depending on your particular product or idea, but the following will get you started:

- Would you buy this product?
- What would you pay for this product?
- What features would you most like to see incorporated within this product?
- Is color important?
- Is the size important?
- Would you buy more than one?

- Would you buy this product as a gift?
- Would you tell friends about this product?
- What advertising would best attract your interest?

The answers to these questions will give you the basic information you need. You can ask many more questions, and if you can afford it, you might want to hire a marketing, survey, and research company that can develop questions and ask hundreds or thousands of people for you.

3.2 Join an inventors' association

You can get excellent marketing information, free assessments, and solid feedback by joining an association of inventors. Most larger cities have inventors' groups. Some are very professional while others are more like hobby groups. Some groups offer professional product assessment or may work with a college or university to offer invention assessments. Look in your telephone directory or ask for help at the local library to find an inventors' group near you.

You can go to a few meetings of these groups for free and determine if you want to become a member. Most groups don't cost much to join and will provide you with a wealth of information, resources, and support. You'll find that members are just like you — creative people trying to market a great idea — and generally people are willing to help each other. Find the successful members in the group and ask them questions. Most will be more than happy to assist you with information on everything from local prototype makers to the best trade shows.

A list of inventors' organizations is included in the appendix on the CD. The list includes members of the United Inventors Association of the USA, a national group with many branches.

4. Refining Your Idea

Once you have determined whether or not the market likes your idea, you need to put that knowledge to work for you. If they love it, congratulations, you are one step closer to success. However, if they are ambivalent about it, or strongly dislike it, it's time to re-evaluate your product.

Look at the assessments of your study group. Try to determine if there are widespread concerns that need to be addressed, or if there is only a small percentage of people with specific concerns. Determine what percentages you think are acceptable. 20 percent is not a lot to worry about, but an 80 percent concern would be hard to ignore.

Refining your product can be a very expensive process. While some inventors will be able to alter a prototype or a design very easily because they are mechanically inclined, others will need to depend on the services of others (see chapter 4 on prototypes and design).

Once you have refined your idea, either by writing a new description or by building a new prototype, you need to test it in the market again. Don't assume that just by making a few changes you're ready to go to market. You can never do enough research or become too educated about the market and your product or idea.

Sometimes it takes several tries to get it right. The more you refine your idea at the beginning, the quicker and easier it will be to get to market.

5. Assessing the Larger Market

Now it's time to go a step further and assess the needs of the larger market. This step will provide you with the information on how much product you think you can sell.

Typically, inventors test their products locally, as this is the easiest and least expensive route. However, you need to be cautious with this approach, and not assume that the local market represents something bigger. Many times I have seen inventors make this mistake, thinking that because their product sells well locally it will do just as well nationally.

One way to determine if your product has national appeal is to use eBay. You can either set up your own account, or try to sell your preliminary product through someone else's account. There are also consumer stores called E-Sell that will take your product and do all the rest, charging a 35 percent commission (which is less mark-up than many retail stores).

Many times the national market is limited only by your ability to produce the quantity needed. If your product is selling well locally, try expanding into a nearby state. The best way to do this is to visit the trade shows in each state, where you can try to develop a relationship with local managers to national chain stores. Since managers have the ability to carry local products as well as national brands, they will pass along local new product discoveries to their national headquarters.

Understanding the size of your market will, of course, affect the design and production. For example, if you determine that you can only sell 1,000 units a year, you may decide that investing in injection tooling or expensive manufacturing tooling is not worth it, even if that is the best way to produce your product.

I like to tell inventors to let the product pay its own way, especially if they are doing their own production and marketing. It's important to understand that the first run may not be as refined as you would like, but that the profits from that first run can provide the money needed to make improvements at a later date. As well, a limited run will help you further assess the market. If you are meeting a public need, you can then expand your market and grow your business. If later you decide to license, the existing sales will make finding a licensing arrangement easier. Or, you may find out that you are happier keeping things small.

I once worked with an inventor from Arkansas, who started selling a new kind of rake he built himself in his garage. He had created a thriving little business and had many retail outlets selling his product. Buoyed by his success, he decided to try to sell the rake to Wal-Mart. The next thing he knew, he was faced with the daunting task of producing 25,000 rakes to fill Wal-Mart's order. After months of problems and almost going bankrupt, this inventor decided he'd rather stay small. He realized that he was happiest working in his garage selling to hardware stores.

This is a typical story, and one to consider when assessing your market. Perhaps there exists a larger market than you are interested in. Many people are perfectly satisfied running a cottage business, without the hassle of dealing with investors, companies that won't pay you for six months, and complex administration. Even a small part-time business can make a lot of money with the right idea. Others would rather not get involved in the day-to-day operations, and for them licensing may be the best option (see chapter 7 for information on licensing).

The remaining chapters of this book consider various approaches to developing your product or idea and getting it to market. But first you have to be sure you are well organized to consider all the possible routes.

6. Getting Organized

If you are serious about taking your idea to market or developing your dream further, you must be organized. That old shoebox full of receipts, drawings, and great ideas is not going to work anymore.

The first thing to do is start a file. If you don't have a file cabinet, start with an inexpensive box file or something similar to hold all the papers relating to your invention.

If you're one of those inventors who have literally hundreds of ideas and are still coming up with more, start another file for those other ideas and future projects, and set it aside. Most importantly, pick one idea to pursue, and only one. Developing an idea for the market is hard enough without distractions.

The first item to put in your file is a written description of your idea. Then make separate folders for information in these categories:

- Marketing, advertising, promotions, sales information

- Prototyping, manufacturing companies, product and material specifications

- Licensing and possible target companies to approach

- Patents, trademarks, copyright information

- Competitors and similar products.

Don't forget that all costs associated with your invention are tax deductible (see chapter 6).

You'll also want to create a logbook for recording revisions and updates to your invention (see chapter 2).

Now you're ready to take the next steps to get your product or idea to market. The remaining chapters of this book will show you the way. Keep in mind, however, that nothing will happen overnight. Taking your product to market requires patience, perseverance, and innovation. But with the knowledge gained here, and a little luck, you will soon be well on your way.

2

How to Protect Your Idea Using Intellectual Property Law

Thomas Alva Edison (1847–1931) started out as a newsboy. He went on to own 1,093 registered patents including those for the phonograph, the light bulb, the alkaline battery, and even the first talking doll, invented in 1888.

Somewhere between the conception of your invention and the marketing of it, you need to protect your idea so that no one else can borrow it and beat you to the market. Protection might be through a patent, trademark or service mark, or copyright registration, all of which fall under the realm of intellectual property law. You may also qualify for trade secret protection.

Intellectual property covers everything from inventions to art. It can include industrial design, ornamental design, processes, trade secrets, music, literary work, films, and even plants. Intellectual property rights have now even been extended to cover genetic engineering, computer software programs, and methods of doing business. Intellectual property is sometimes referred to as intangible property, proprietary assets, industrial property or proprietary rights.

Typically, if you have an idea or an improvement to an idea that involves a mechanical, electrical, or chemical process, you most likely will want patent protection. If your idea involves written material such as a book, article, written instruction, or recipe, you most likely want copyright protection. Logos and sayings that are associated with marketing a product are covered under trademarks or service marks.

Not all products can or should be protected. Many new products are produced and put on the market successfully each year without any intellectual property protection. Some inventions fall into what is known as the public domain, which means that everybody has a right to the use and or manufacture of these products. Public domain products are products that were patented long ago and the patents have run out, or products that cannot be patented either because they were already in common use or they were not unique enough to have ever received a patent. Many patents today are simply improvements on existing public domain.

This chapter discusses the various types of protection available and gives the basic information you need to make the best decision for you and your product. You may find that your new product or invention requires *all* forms of intellectual property protection. For example, my first invention, the Fire Guardian, had both US and foreign patents to protect the mechanical process. The name of the product was trademarked, and the written advertisements were copyrighted.

1. Basic Protection: Keeping a Logbook

Creating a paper trail is one of the oldest and least expensive ways of protecting your invention. All you need is a simple inventor's logbook. The ideal logbook is bound or stitched so its pages cannot be removed or altered. A loose-leaf notebook will not work. A daily planner, which you can purchase at any stationery or business supply store, makes a good inventor's logbook.

The logbook, properly maintained, can be used as documentation in the event of a legal dispute, and therefore should not be taken lightly. In it you can record the date of conception, test results, successful prototypes, and failures. If you decide to use an inventor's logbook, you should start it as soon as possible after the idea is conceived. A well-kept logbook will include your thoughts, sketches, notes, calculations, telephone numbers, and contacts.

For the logbook to stand up in court (should it ever come to that), the documentation must be presented in such a way that anyone reading it can easily understand and comprehend the information. Once an invention is described in detail, you should date and sign the appropriate page or pages, and have your signature notarized or witnessed. (If it seems risky to you to have your logbook notarized because you are exposing your idea, remember that the notary is merely witnessing your signature and the date, and does not need to see or understand the information contained in your logbook regarding your invention.)

Even if you never have to use your logbook for legal matters, its importance cannot be understated or diminished. Sometimes going back six months in the logbook to locate an old telephone number or contact can have real value in itself.

Here are a few guidelines for maintaining a high-quality logbook:

- Keep a separate logbook for each project you work on and make notes each time you work on your invention.

- Once your idea is developed to some potential, describe it and have the description notarized or witnessed.

- Keep all records such as telephone numbers, contacts, addresses, notes, tests, and any reference material in your logbook.

- Do not leave blank pages. Use your logbook chronologically to maintain its validity.

- When demonstrating a prototype to a witness, have the witness give a written description of the operation and the results observed. The witness should then sign and date the appropriate page or pages.

Remember that keeping a logbook is a common practice of engineers, designers, and research and development personnel who want to protect their ideas by maintaining clear and accurate records of their genesis and progress.

2. Disclosure Document Program

An alternative or additional protection to the logbook is offered by the disclosure document program. This program is inexpensive and allows you to file your idea at the patent office.

The program is administered by the United States Patent and Trademark Office, which accepts and preserves your invention disclosure document in strict confidence for a period of two years, or longer if your patent application refers to the disclosure. The purpose of this service is to provide a credible form of evidence, should you need it.

Originally, this service was intended to stop inventors from mailing a description of their own inventions to themselves, which many mistakenly believe to be a valid form of protection (sometimes called the poor man's patent).

The disclosure document is not a substitute for a patent application and should not be considered a grace period for filing the application. The program is aimed at allowing inventors to feel protected enough to proceed with their ideas, rather than hiding or sitting on them. Just like an inventor's logbook, a disclosure document can be upheld in court and can ultimately resolve a patent infringement case.

To file a disclosure document, follow these steps:

1. Prepare, on an 8 1/2 by 11 sheet of paper (or a copy from your logbook), a description of your invention. The description must be limited to written matter or drawings on paper or other thin, flexible material such as linen, plastic, or Mylar, having dimensions or folded to dimensions not to exceed 8 1/2 by 13 inches.

2. Number each page. Text and drawings should be sufficiently dark and bold to permit reproduction with commonly used office copy machines. Photographs may be submitted, but they are not required. Although not a requirement, you can have the disclosure document notarized.

3. Send your description, along with a check or money order for $20 payable to the Commission of Patents and Trademarks, Box DD, Assistant Commissioner, Washington, DC, 20231. Include a stamped, self-addressed envelope and the following signed request in duplicate:

    The undersigned, being the inventor of the disclosed invention, requests that the enclosed papers be accepted under the disclosure document program and that they be preserved for a period of two years.

When received by the Patent and Trademark Office, your disclosure document will be stamped with an identification number and the date of receipt. The duplicate request will then be returned to you in the self-addressed envelope together with a notice indicating that the disclosure document may be relied upon only as evidence, and that a patent application should be filed if patent protection is desired.

The disclosure document program does not diminish the value of your notarized and witnessed records as evidence of the conception date of your invention. It does, however, provide the Patent and Trademark Office with a credible form of evidence which can be referred to in a separate letter in the patent application, should you decide to file within the two-year period.

There is also an online service available that will record conception of an idea for a fee (see <www.firstuse.com>). However, this method has never been tested in court.

3. Patents

3.1 Understanding patents

A patent is an exclusive grant giving its owner, the patentee, the right to exclude others from making, selling, and sometimes even using the invention as defined in the specifications and claims of the patent. As of 1996, these rights also can exclude others from offering for sale within or importing into the United States.

Generally, a patent lasts for 20 years unless the patent application was filed before June 8, 1995. In this case, the grant is for 17 years from the date the patent was issued. Both the 17- and 20-year periods can be extended up to five years in certain instances. To maintain a patent, maintenance fees must be paid every three-and-a-half years.

While patents are considered a grant or contract with the government, they actually offer no rights at all. Patents do offer the right to keep others from using or selling the patented invention, but they do not offer the monopoly many believe to coexist with patents.

There are three basic types of patents available today: utility patents, design patents, and living plant patents.

3.1a Utility patents

Utility patents are by far the most common of all patents and protect everything from new machinery to genetically altered animals. There are hundreds of categories for utility patents, covering items such as hardware, toys, tools, vehicles, sporting goods, time/labor saving devices, and cooking implements.

If your invention relates to a functional aspect of any machine, process, method, article, or composition, the best method of protection is the utility patent.

3.1b Design patents

A design patent is only applicable to esthetics or ornamental features; the design in itself may have no significant functional purpose. The design must be inseparable from the invention and cannot be a surface ornamentation, such as a cover or label. To qualify as a design patent, your invention's appearance must not be obvious — that is, someone with ordinary skills in your field could not easily design the same appearance.

A good example of a design that could be patented is a tire tread design. The tread offers a design feature to the tire, which by itself would not be patentable. The design patent on the tread would protect your invention from infringers using any similar designs.

Because many past inventors have used design patents when their inventions did not qualify for a utility patent, design patents have the reputation as being second-rate, but this is not true. Design patents are not only easier to apply for and receive, but are far less costly than utility patents. A typical design patent application fee is $170, and there are no maintenance fees.

Design patents allow the same rights as utility patents, but the patent term is only 14 years instead of 20. Design patents allow you to use the patent pending status and to license your invention. Design patent applications consist of a drawing, appropriate forms, and a filing fee if you are an individual inventor or small company.

3.1c Plant patents

Plant patents cover all new varieties of plants produced asexually from cutting and grafting and, unlike utility patents, usefulness is not a requirement for patentability. One of the better-known plant patents is for the peach, invented by Luther Burbank, who also invented the Burbank potato (introduced into Ireland to help combat the blight epidemic). Burbank invented more than 800 new strains of plums, prunes, berries, and lilies. Plant patents, though rare, are still very important to today's agricultural market.

3.2 Qualifying for a patent

The patent law, United States Code Title 35-101, says:

> *Whoever invents or discovers any new and useful process, machine, manufacture, or composition of matter, or any new and useful improvement thereof, may obtain a patent thereof, subject to the conditions and requirements of this title.*

The law further dictates these conditions for patentability:

- The invention cannot be known or used by others, or patented or described in a printed publication anywhere before the inventor applies for a patent.

- The invention cannot be used in public or be on sale for more than one year prior to application for a patent.

- The invention cannot be abandoned in another application.

- The invention cannot already be patented for more than one year in a foreign country.

- The invention cannot be described in another patent or application.

- The invention cannot be invented by someone else.

If two inventions are filed at the same time, the patent office will consider not only the respective dates of conception and the reduction to practice, but also the reasonable diligence of who was first to put the invention into practice. In other words, the patent office will evaluate who actually did the most to commercialize the invention. (Note that the United States is the only country that awards patents to the first to conceive, not the first to patent.)

The following are *not* patentable:

- An idea

- A method of doing business

- Subject matter that falls under trademarks or copyright

- Inoperable devices such as perpetual motion machines, without working prototypes

- An obvious improvement, such as using plastic to replace steel

- Illegal inventions such as a money-making machine or a new safe-cracking explosive

- Nuclear weapons

- Theoretical matters, such as the big bang theory

- Untested drugs, which require FDA approval to be patentable

A patent application must originally be filed in the name of the actual inventor. However, patent rights may be assigned, licensed, or even given away. Assignments must be in writing and must be recorded in the US Patent and Trademark Office within three months of the assignment. In an employment situation, if the employee is hired to invent specific subject matter, any patent obtained on such subject matter would be owned by the employer. Many employees sign contracts that specifically provide for ownership of all patent rights.

3.3 How to apply for a patent

To obtain a patent, you must file an application with the federal government asking that it find the subject matter described in the application new, useful, and unobvious. Your application must be filed within one year after the invention is first placed in public use, disclosed in a printed publication, or placed on sale. If you do not file within a year, you will have lost your right to file.

A patent application consists of these items:

- The title of your invention

- Background or history of the invention

- The invention's features, advantages, and objectives

- A brief description of the drawings
- A narrative description of the structure
- An explanation of how the invention works
- A summary of claims
- Drawings
- A filing fee (either check or money order)
- A transmittal (cover) letter
- A stamped, self-addressed receipt postcard
- A completed Patent Application Declaration
- An Information Disclosure Statement
- Copies of patents you cited in your application and listed on the Information Disclosure Statement

To file for a patent, you can contact a patent agent or attorney to assist you or you can do it yourself. A patent attorney will charge you $5,000 to $10,000, but cannot guarantee that a patent will be issued. However, an attorney is familiar with the procedures and will ensure that everything is done correctly. To find a good patent attorney, check with your local inventors' association.

A word of warning: avoid the services of so-called inventor assistance groups that offer to prepare your patent application for a fee, usually for much less than what a patent agent or attorney would charge. These services may end up costing you a great deal of money and accomplish little. Although it would be unfair to assume that all invention brokers are of questionable character, many are more concerned about profit from inventors than profit from inventions. Use common sense when choosing any business associate.

If you choose to file your own patent, you should learn as much about the process as you can. One very good book on the topic is *Patent It Yourself*, by David Pressman (Nolo Press). If you have the skill to write about things of a technical nature, you may find that writing a patent application is enjoyable.

The forms required for filing a patent application can be obtained from the patent office or the library's book of forms.

Keep in mind that the process of filing and receiving patent approval can take a long time. Depending on the circumstances, a design patent, for example, can take up to 18 months to obtain and a utility patent can take up to two-and-a-half years to obtain.

Writing a patent application can be an art form all its own, and it should be well researched in order to be effective. This following example is from an actual patent. See if you can guess what it's really saying.

> The cells of the web each have a cross section comprising a convoluted swale in a radial reverse anticline and agonic configuration. Said configuration furthermore having a primary rhomoid anticline section and a plurality of preferably substantially identical angularly disposed radially outwardly extending swale stile in a configuration complementary to the configuration anticline of primary centrally disposed primary section for dihedral prolaped engagement facilitating a nesting communication providing a supported lagging stile whereas radially outwardly extending swale provide both improved strength and manufacturing improvements.
>
> This is a description of a series of honeycomb cells.

3.4 Provisional patent application

As of June 8, 1995, the US Patent Office now accepts provisional patent applications for purposes of establishing a priority date for the invention. The provisional patent application was designed to establish an early filing date for a regular patent application filed within a year.

Under this system, an inventor who files a provisional patent application has up to 12 months in which to file a formal application and still claim priority based on the filing date of the provisional application.

A provisional application requires only a detailed description with one claim, although more than one claim can be written. A drawing is required, but it doesn't have to be as detailed as for a regular patent drawing. Further, the only form that needs to be filed is the provisional application cover sheet.

A provisional application can save you over $300 in application fees and offer patent pending status as well.

A provisional application can be a good choice with an invention that is affected by rapidly changing technology. A provisional patent application would allow patent pending status while testing a quickly changing market, giving you the flexibility to either continue with a regular application within the one-year time limit or determining if the invention is viable.

However, you should understand that a provisional patent application cannot turn into a provisional patent and will not mature into a granted patent without further submissions. A provisional patent application must be followed by a non-provisional application that requires additional fees, forms, and specifications.

Additionally, provisional patent applications are not examined on their merits.

The benefits of the provisional application cannot be claimed if the one-year deadline for filing a non-provisional application has expired. Provisional applications cannot claim the benefit of a previously filed application, either foreign or domestic.

A provisional patent application should be mailed to:

Mail Stop Patent Application
Commissioner for Patents
PO Box 1450
Alexandria, VA 22313-1450

3.5 Filing and processing costs

A typical utility patent application can take at least two years to obtain and will cost $385 or more. See the Appendix and CD for the complete and latest patent fees. You can also visit <www.uspto.gov/> for the latest price increases. Fees can be raised each year, typically in October.

3.6 Simplified small entity status

Another consideration when applying for a patent is choosing small entity status. To qualify for small entity status you must be an independent inventor and/or a company with less than 500 employees. If you qualify, all fees are reduced by 50 percent. This status can also allow for special consideration for financing and government grants (discussed in later chapters).

You can establish small entity status simply by writing to assert your entitlement to it. You do this by checking the box on the appropriate forms describing yourself (or your business) as a small entity status.

3.7 Patent searches

Before you file a patent application, even if you are hiring an attorney or patent agent, it is always advisable to conduct a patent search first. The patent search is your insurance against spending time and money unnecessarily. When doing your patent search, you will either become more aware of just how brilliant your idea really is, or you will discover that there are different versions of your idea already patented (called "prior art"). Of course, finding similar prior art is not necessarily bad news. The education you get from reviewing other inventions should only assist you in further developing your own invention.

There are two ways to conduct a patent search. One is to do an online search at the US Patent and Trademark Office (USPTO) website. The other is to do a patent library search. The latter is a little more trouble, but it is much more hands-on and educational.

3.7a Online USPTO searches

On the main USPTO website <www.uspto.gov>, you can conduct a search for free. This is a wonderful tool for investigating the possibilities of getting a patent, of simply for educating yourself as to how many patents may exist on an idea. It is a simple means for gaining some very detailed information.

Start by using the keyword search to see just how much activity falls within your search realm. Try every combination of words because some topics will not show up until you hit on a particular combination. Using simple Boolean terms (key words), you will easily determine if others have patented the same or similar ideas to yours.

Be sure to review the prior art references on the patents you find. This information can be enlightening because it shows what patent examiners thought was relevant to those applications.

Do not let the fact that other patents exist deter you from proceeding on your course. When I first did a patent search, I was disappointed to see that my idea had been patented in the 1800s. Yet

I still received a patent for my improvements and later licensed it in several countries because of my improvements to the prior art.

3.7b Patent library searches

There are patent libraries in each state, and you can find the one nearest you by consulting the Appendix and CD . If you choose this route, you must first understand the patent classification system and determine which class and subclass your invention falls into.

The US Patent and Trademark Office maintains a highly sophisticated classification system, arranging patents into hundreds of subject classes and more than 100,000 subclasses in chronological order dating back to 1790. You can begin searching by looking through the Patent Office Manual of Classification (available at your public library) or on the Internet at <www.uspto.gov.> You can also purchase the manual in loose-leaf form, by writing to the Superintendent of Documents, US Government Printing Office, Washington, DC.

Alternatively, you can take advantage of the free service offered to inventors by the patent office to help find their class and subclass, but you have to wait three to eight weeks to receive a response. If you do choose this route, simply write your name and address at the top of an 8 1/2 x 11 sheet of paper. Below that write: "Please advise me what subject area and/or class(es) and/or subclass(es) cover my intended invention." Then list your invention's features, operation, and intended use. Give accurate details, so that your idea is fully understood; otherwise you may be given an incorrect class or subclass. Once completed, mail the information to:

Commissioner of Patents and Trademarks
PO Box 1450
Alexandria, VA 22313-1450

Once you have determined your class and subclass, go to the patent library nearest you and ask for a computer listing of all patents in your class. You will be given a list of the patents in which you need to search. The patents are listed chronologically, beginning with the newest. A "D" beside a patent indicates it is a design patent, an "X" indicates a cross-reference, and "R.E" indicates a reissue.

Now you can start your search by examining the abstracts in the Official Gazette, a weekly publication that lists the patents issued for that week, grouped by general, mechanical, chemical, electrical, design, and reissued patents. This publication offers a means for viewing a summary of the invention, known as an abstract. Along with the abstract there will also be a drawing, where possible. This abstract allows a more efficient search without your having to dig through the mountains of paperwork on the 5 million-plus US patents.

In some libraries you may give the librarian the list of relevant patents, and he or she will make copies of them, usually at a nominal charge. Many librarians may simply direct you to the patent files and copying machine to make your own copies, so be sure to take with you a pocketful of change. If cost is not an issue and you have the time, the list may also be sent to the Patent and Trademark Office for copies at the prevailing rates.

One word of warning: Doing a patent search in a patent library can take a long time. Be prepared to stay awhile, and don't take shortcuts by scanning relevant patents. This may come back to haunt you later. Remember, it is easier to do it right the first time than make an additional trip later.

3.8 Patent pending status

That stage between sending in the patent application and possibly receiving a patent requires special considerations. If you are proceeding with the marketing of your invention, the only legal protection you can obtain is the patent pending label. This label legally warns would-be patent infringers that a patent has been applied for and may be granted. If, however, you are tempted to use the patent pending label without first filing an application, you can be fined for this federal offense.

Patent pending status is both a marketing tool and a bluff. You have no rights to stop others from making your invention while you are applying for a patent. You could write a letter to the would-be infringer and warn him or her that when you receive your patent, you will sue. However, that person could write a similar letter to you after filing his or her own patent application. The point is to put your faith in the invention and not the possible patent. If your plan is to license your invention, remember that an existing market has more bargaining power than a proposed patent.

While your invention is pending patent, explore the market, even if only in a limited fashion. You will find when approaching the marketplace that your invention will evolve according to market influences. In some cases, the market influences the invention so much that the original patent is abandoned, and a new invention is created and patented.

Depending on the invention, new improvements needed for marketing your invention can even be incorporated into an existing patent application. During the process, your claims may be amended and strengthened, sometimes even allowing new subject matter, if done properly.

4. Trademarks and Service Marks

4.1 What is a trademark or service mark?

If your creation includes any written or artistic matter that includes a symbol, word, shape, or design, and you use this mark as a brand name, service mark, or trade dress, you qualify for protection under trademark law.

Trademarks are used by manufacturers or merchants to identify goods, and to distinguish them from those goods manufactured or sold by others. A trademark can be obtained as easily as affixing the symbol ™ to your mark, or you can register it with the federal trademark office and use the symbol ®. Many people consider trademarks a brand name and will buy products based upon their former experiences with a certain trademark.

Service marks are sometimes confused with trademarks, but they are actually slogans or phrases used in the sale or advertising of services rather than products. Service marks identify the services of one person or company and distinguish them from the services of others. For example, the use of the slogan "We print it in a minute" by a printing business indicates the type of services rendered to its customers. Service marks and trademarks are registered in the same way.

4.2 Protection offered

A trademark only protects you from people using a similar mark on their goods, which could cause confusion. A trademark of an anchor for a line of boats, for example, could in fact be registered again for a line of clothes. But if you were selling a line of boats, you could not modify someone's trademark of an anchor and use it yourself.

If a trademark is federally registered in the US Patent and Trademark Office, the ® symbol, or the words "Registered in the US Patent and Trademark Office," must be used. Failure to give this notice prevents you from recovering damages for trademark infringement.

If your trademark or service mark is not registered federally or is registered only in your state, a ™ or ℠ is used to identify this condition. The ™ or ℠ symbol must be smaller than the actual trademark and must follow the mark. (Before deciding on a size for your symbol, you may wish to look at other marks found on other goods, to get a feel for such things as artwork and the size comparison between the trademark and the symbol.)

A US federal trademark registration lasts for ten years, but can be renewed in perpetuity. There are different requirements in each state for trademarks to remain valid. Typically, the requirement is its use within the industry.

4.3 Conditions for registration

A trademark is owned by the first person or company to use the mark in commerce, meaning whoever first uses it in public is considered the owner of the mark, whether the mark is registered or not. Therefore, before you can register a trademark, you have to show that the mark is not recorded as belonging to another person or organization. That is why it is advisable when applying for a federal trademark to have a search done, although it is not necessary for state registration.

Another condition is that it must not resemble another mark or be of a content so as to confuse or deceive a buyer. For example, a trademark of "China Fashions" for clothes designed and manufactured in Oklahoma would most likely be refused registration. This condition should be considered if you intend to start with a state trademark and later obtain a federal trademark. Your marketing power could be damaged by having to change your logo midstream.

After meeting these conditions, a trademark can be obtained and even licensed. Your trademark is intellectual property, and you have the right to use it and even seek protection from the courts if someone else tries to infringe on it.

4.4 The value of a trademark

Trademarks should never be underestimated as a marketing tool for product success. Can you imagine going to a store and finding products on the shelves without brand names? The inferior products would look exactly the same as the superior products. It wouldn't be long before the better manufacturers lost all incentive to maintain their high-quality standards, because they would not enjoy greater sales for their extra efforts.

Trademarks are an important part of a person's decision to purchase a product. If you bought a brand-name refrigerator that worked well, you would be more inclined to purchase a stove by the same company, even though they are entirely different products. A company's reputation can make a future product successful simply through its trademark.

In cases where the product is sold directly to the consumer, the trademark is extremely valuable. For example, if I knew the formula for Coca-Cola and sold it on the market under a different name, many people would say it had a different taste, and most Coca-Cola drinkers would not even try it at all because the consumer has come to rely on certain manufacturers for quality. Once the quality of your product gains a name for itself, others will have the same trouble getting people away from your product to try theirs.

Remember, however, that with your trademark also comes a responsibility to maintain adequate quality control. The value of a trademark is that the public sees it as an exclusive sign of a business, and bad news often travels faster than good news.

4.5 What you cannot trademark

These are the types of material that cannot be trademarked:

- Immoral, scandalous, or deceptive matter
- Trade names
- Slogans
- Governmental emblems

- Personal names
- Marks that may cause confusion
- A person's likeness, without that person's consent
- Geographical locations
- Descriptive words
- Generic words

4.6 The trademark application

A federal trademark application is comprised of these items:

- A written application form
- A drawing of the work
- Three specimens showing actual use of the mark in connection with the goods or service
- The required filing fee (currently $335)

The written application form must be in English and include a heading to identify the mark, a class number, and specify if you are an individual, corporation, or partnership.

To receive the appropriate forms and information to federally register a trademark, write to:

US **Patent and Trademark Office**
Office of Public Affairs
Washington, DC 20231

Or

Office of Independent Inventor Programs
Crystal Park 2, Suite 0100
Washington, DC 20231

Or go online at <www.uspto.gov>.

Indicate in your letter whether you wish to apply on the basis of actual use or intent to use, and specify whether you're an individual, corporation, or partnership.

The US Patent Office provides an electronic search system called TESS, which contains more than 2.9 million pending, registered, and dead federal trademarks. For online searching, go to <www.tess.uspto.gov>.

The patent office now allows you to file your trademark applications online using (TEAS) Trademark Electronic Application System. You can also use (PrinTEAS) to print out the completed forms for mailing to the USPTO.

Unlike patents, trademarks have an indefinite life when used properly. Federal trademarks are issued for 10 years and can be renewed if still in use.

If you wish to register a trademark in your state, call or write to your secretary of state for forms and instructions. The cost varies from state to state and can range from $25 to $100.

4.7 Filing and processing costs

Generally an application fee for a federal trademark will cost $335 or more. State registered trademarks will cost about $50 and can be registered with your Secretary of State.

You can obtain the latest information on fees for trademark applications by visiting the government website at <www.uspto.gov>.

5. Copyright

5.1 What is copyright?

Copyright is a form of protection to authors of original works of authorship, including literary, dramatic, musical, artistic, and certain other intellectual works. Copyright is obtained the minute the work assumes some tangible form, and it lasts for 50 years after the creator's death. This protection is available to both published and unpublished works and generally gives the owner of a copyright the exclusive right to do and to authorize others to:

- Reproduce the work
- Prepare derivative works
- Distribute copies of the work
- Transfer ownership, by rental, lease, or lending
- Perform the work publicly
- Display the copyrighted work publicly

Of all the methods of intellectual properly protection, copyright is probably the most misunderstood. For example, many people believe that for copyright to be effective, a copyright notice is required. While the copyright notice will strengthen the protection of your copyright and even allow you to get more and different damages in court, it is not necessary.

Another misconception is that you can use someone else's copyrighted material as long as you don't re-sell it for profit. In fact anything that damages the copyright holder is a violation.

Many website developers would have you believe that anything on the Internet is public domain. Website design is especially prone to copyright violation, but because the industry is still new, many laws are only now being reviewed and changed to protect companies on the Net.

5.2 Who can claim copyright?

Copyright protection begins from the time the work is created in any fixed form. Generally, the copyright is the property of the author who created the work. The authors of a joint work are co-owners of the copyright, unless there is an agreement to the contrary. Copyright in each separate contribution to a periodical or other collective work is distinct from copyright in the collective work as a whole and vests initially with the author of the contribution.

In the case of works "made for hire" (i.e., work prepared by an employee within the scope of his or her employment), the copyright holder is the employer, not the employee.

5.3 What can be protected by copyright?

Copyright protects original works of authorship that are fixed in a tangible form. Copyrightable works include the following:

- Literary works

- Musical works, including any accompanying words

- Dramatic works, including any accompanying music

- Pantomimes and choreographic works

- Pictorial, graphic, and sculptural works

- Motion pictures and other audiovisual works

- Sound recordings

- Architectural works

These categories should be viewed broadly. For example, computer programs and most compilations may be registered as literary works, while maps and architectural plans may be registered as pictorial, graphic, and sculptural works.

5.4 What is not protected by copyright?

These categories of material are generally not eligible for federal copyright protection:

- Works that have not been fixed in a tangible form of expression (e.g., choreographic works that have not been notated or recorded, or improvisational speeches or performances that have not been written or recorded)

- Titles, names, short phrases, and slogans

- Familiar symbols or designs

- Mere variations of typographic ornamentation, lettering, or coloring

- Mere listings of ingredients or contents

- Ideas, procedures, methods, systems, processes, concepts, principles, discoveries, or devices, as distinguished from a description, explanation, or illustration

Works consisting entirely of information that is common property and containing no original authorship such as standard calendars, height and weight charts, tape measures and rulers, and lists or tables taken from public documents or other common sources are also not able to be copyrighted.

5.5 Using the copyright notice

You do not have to use a copyright notice to claim copyright, although doing so can be beneficial. (Before 1989, when the United States adhered to the Berne Convention, using a notice was required, so it is still relevant to the copyright status of older works.)

Use of the notice may be important because it informs the public that the work is protected by copyright, it identifies the copyright owner, and it shows the year of first publication. Furthermore, if the work is infringed on, use of the notice can protect you against someone claiming that he or she "innocently infringed" on the copyright. (Innocent infringement occurs when the infringer did not realize that the work was protected.)

The use of the copyright notice is the responsibility of the copyright owner and does not require permission from, or registration with, the Copyright Office. The notice must contain the following three elements:

- The copyright symbol ©, or the word "Copyright," or the abbreviation "Copr.";

- The year of first publication of the work; and

- The name of the owner of copyright in the work, or an abbreviation by which the name can be recognized, or a generally known alternative designation of the owner.

An example of a copyright notice incorporating these three elements is:

© 2005 Quest International

5.6 How long does copyright protection last?

Under the current law, a work is automatically protected from the moment of its creation, and ordinarily lasts for 70 years after the author's death. For works made for hire, copyright lasts 95 years from publication or 120 years from creation, whichever is shorter.

5.7 Copyright registration

In general, copyright registration is a legal formality intended to make a public record of the basic facts of a particular copyright. Registration is not a condition of copyright protection, but it does provide some advantages to copyright owners. These are some of the advantages:

- Registration establishes a public record of the copyright claim.

- Before an infringement suit may be filed in court, registration is necessary for works of US origin.

- If made before or within five years of publication, registration will establish evidence in court of the validity of the copyright and of the facts stated in the certificate.

- If registration is made within three months after publication of the work or prior to an infringement of the work, statutory damages and attorney's fees will be available to the copyright owner in court actions. Otherwise, only an award of actual damages and profits is available to the copyright owner.

- Registration allows the owner of the copyright to record the registration with the US Customs Service for protection against the importation of infringing copies.

To register a work, you must send a properly completed application form, the copyright fee, and a non-returnable deposit of the work being registered *in the same envelope or package* to:

Library of Congress
Copyright Office
101 Independence Avenue, SE
Washington, DC 20540

You can download the forms you need from the Copyright Office website at <www.copyright.gov forms>. Print the forms head to head (top of page 2 is directly behind the top of page 1) on a single piece of good quality, 8-1/2-inch by 11-inch white paper. To achieve the best-quality copies of the application forms, use a laser printer.

Your copyright registration will be effective on the date the Copyright Office receives all the required elements in acceptable form, regardless of how long it takes to process the application and mail the certificate of registration. The time required to process an application varies, depending on the amount of material the Copyright Office is receiving.

If you apply for copyright registration, you will not receive an acknowledgment that your application has been received (the Copyright Office receives more than 600,000 applications annually), but you can expect —

- a letter or telephone call from a Copyright Office staff member if further information is needed, or

- a certificate of registration indicating that the work has been registered, or if the application cannot be accepted, a letter explaining why it has been rejected.

Requests to have certificates available for pickup at the Copyright Public Information Office or to have certificates sent by Federal Express or another mail service cannot be honored. If you want to know the date that the Copyright Office receives your material, send it by registered or certified mail and request a return receipt.

5.8 Registration fees

You must remit the registration fee by check, money order, or bank draft, payable to Register of Copyrights. Do not send cash. Drafts must be redeemable without service or exchange fee through a US institution, must be payable in US dollars, and must be imprinted with American Banking Association routing numbers. If a check received in payment of the filing fee is returned to the copyright office as uncollectible, the Copyright Office will cancel the registration and will notify you.

Typically, the standard fee is $30. For current information on fees for basic registration, document recordation, supplementary registration, search services, certificates, and additional certificates, call the Copyright Public Information Office at (202) 707-3000, 8:30 a.m. to 5:00 p.m. Eastern time, Monday through Friday, except federal holidays.

Or, you may write for information to:

Library of Congress
Copyright Office
101 Independence Avenue, SE
Washington, DC 20559-6000

5.9 Mandatory deposit for works published in the United States

Although a copyright registration is not required, the Copyright Act establishes a mandatory deposit requirement for works published in the United States. In general, the owner of copyright or the owner of the exclusive right of publication in the work has a legal obligation to deposit in the Copyright Office, within three months of publication, two copies for the use of the Library of Congress.

Failure to make the deposit can result in fines and other penalties but does not affect copyright protection. I have never heard of anyone being fined, but this could be an issue if you are in court protecting your rights.

For works published in the United States, the copyright law contains a provision under which a single deposit can be made to satisfy both the deposit requirements for the Library of Congress and the registration requirements. In order to have this dual effect, the copies must be accompanied by the prescribed application form and filing fee.

6. Trade Secrets

To qualify for a trade secret, you must have information not known by the public that gives you or your company an advantage. Trade secrets include techniques, designs, materials, processes, and formulas. If you have an idea or information you wish to keep secret, you would qualify for trade secret protection.

The concept of the trade secret was developed by the judicial system to protect formulas and other manufacturing secrets. In contrast to patents, which usually last 17 years, a trade secret lasts as long as you can keep it a secret. Patents also require a disclosure of the formulas and technologies involved, which can be duplicated. Of course, trade secrets are not as easy to duplicate, due to the fact they are kept secret.

The most famous example of a trade secret is the formula for Coca-Cola. The basic ingredients are readily identified as water, sugar, caramel coloring, and carbonation; however, the exact quantities and cooking process are masked in mystery and locked away in a high-security vault. If patented, the formula would be made public, and anyone could send for a copy of the patent, and even try to modify and improve it. The Coca-Cola formula will probably remain a trade secret years after an actual patent would have expired.

An idea need not be patentable in order to receive trade secret protection, nor is novelty a requirement. Trade secrets can cover the entire range of business practices. The Uniform Trade Secrets Act safeguards trade secrets if three conditions are met:

- The trade secret must have economic value. This can be any proprietary information including formulas, techniques, pricing information, sales forecasts, and customer information that would give another person or company a competitive advantage.

- Trade secrets must be secret, or unknown to the public, and difficult to uncover.

- The owner of a trade secret must attempt to protect it. If you have employees, they must be made aware of its secrecy. Furthermore, any visiting sales representatives, vendors, customers, inspectors, or the like must be informed of its secrecy if they must access such information.

3

Researching — Making Your Idea Even Better

In 1909, the American Chemist L.H. Baekeland invented Bakelite and started the plastic revolution. Within 40 years of his development, plastic began replacing wood, metal, and glass.

1. Why Research?

Information is power. The more information you have about your idea or invention, the more likely you will be successful against the competition. Without information, your potential is limited.

One inventor once asked me for information on how to sell some specialized clothing she had invented. I consulted the *Directory of Conventions* and referred her to a list of fashion trade shows for her specific interest that are held throughout the United States. I also suggested she look in the library phone books for wholesalers in areas such as Los Angeles and New York. Not having this simple information was holding her back. A little research opened the gates to success and she went on to sell her products nationally.

Learn from this lesson: If your invention fails for lack of information, you have no one to blame but yourself. Researching your invention's potential is simply a sound investment of your time.

As you read further, you will discover that doing research can enhance virtually all aspects of your invention's development. For example, as you learned in the previous chapter, you need to do a patent search to determine if the invention is already in use. You also need to do marketing searches to determine if you have any competitors and whether other markets may be available to you. You can determine demographics, trends, and sales potential by doing research.

Research can be used in many ways to your real advantage. It can —

- assist you in finding similar products already in the marketplace or in finding the parts you need to make your own product,

- teach you about new processes that may need to be utilized in your product's development, and

- tell you where to market your product.

Although it can be time-consuming and laborious, research is an important way of strengthening your armor when being questioned by a potential licensee. When it comes time to license or market your invention, any lack of knowledge on your part will become apparent. A little research now can help you avoid appearing unprepared and uninformed later on.

Between the library and the Internet, almost every kind of information is obtainable. If you don't have access to a computer and the Internet, go to the library and work on a computer there. Consider the time spent researching as an investment in your invention. And it's something you can easily do yourself. I have spoken to many inventors who have paid over $1,000 to so-called invention marketing companies to do their research for them, only to come away disappointed. The information supplied is usually the type that the inventors could have found themselves if they had invested a few hours on the resources readily and easily available to them.

2. The Library — A Researcher's Best Friend

The library is always your best first stop, as it provides a wealth of information for any kind of research. When doing library research, remember these basic guidelines:

- Libraries work in systems. No library has everything, but collectively there are endless possibilities.

- Don't judge a library by its size. All libraries have something to offer, including the services of the librarian.

- When working with librarians, your right to confidentiality is assured.

- Libraries offer professional guidance and will assist you in a variety of search strategies.

- Take the time to browse, especially in the reference sections.

Depending on what particular information you are looking for at any one time, different types of libraries may be more helpful.

- University and college libraries serve the research needs of scholars, students, and researchers, and they have a large number of professional-level books. Although many want to limit their use to faculty and students, most university libraries will allow you access to use their resources. Some, however, will require you to buy a membership for use.

- Large companies such as the Automobile Club of Southern California, Twentieth Century-Fox motion picture studio, Hallmark Cards, and Pillsbury Co. have extensive libraries, generally to help employees perform their duties more efficiently. There may be a large company near you that can help in your research.

- Many large newspaper libraries have reference book and magazine collections for their staff to use in verifying information, and they may allow you to use these resources. Check with the newspaper's editor or publisher.

Libraries have information to assist your marketing that includes listings of hospitals and clinics, federal and state government agencies, consulates and embassies, chambers of commerce, trade professionals and hobby associations, periodicals, government documents, online databases, and local experts.

Libraries also keep resources on all local events, companies, and people right in your neighborhood — such as prototype makers, inventor groups, marketing companies, sales reps, and more.

Several directories are available that identify libraries of every kind and can point you in the right direction in any research endeavor. Again, you'll usually find these directories in the library.

For example, Jaques Cattell Press/R. R. Bowker Co. produce an annual volume that lists more than 30,000 US and Canadian libraries of every imaginable kind. The *Directory of Special Libraries and Information Centers* (Gale Research Co.) has a five-volume set that also compiles a list of libraries.

Other directories that may be of interest include the *Research Centers Directory*, also published by Gale Research Co., and the *Directory of Historical Societies and Agencies in the United States and Canada*. Additionally, the *Subject Collection Directory*, by Lee Ash (R. R. Bowker Co.), lists 7,000 academic, public, museum, and historical society libraries nationwide.

Another helpful directory is the *Writer's Resource Guide* (Writer's Digest Books), which lists resources such as foundations, associations, and agencies that can be helpful in doing research.

3. Using Directories

Once you've narrowed down where you are going to do your research, you can then look at specific directories in your field of interest. The following resources, particularly helpful for inventors, are generally available at most libraries:

3.1 Manufacturers' directories

The following directories may well be your most important resource as an inventor or product developer. They can assist you in finding companies that make similar products or component parts for your product. They are loaded with toll-free numbers to call for free samples, product specifications, and information on the size and worth of companies throughout the United States and Canada. No matter what you're looking for, you will find it in one of these directories.

- *10-K Report*

- *Annual Reports*

- *MacRae's Blue Book*

- *Moody's Manuals*

- *Standard & Poor's Corporation Records*

- *State Directories*

- *Thomas Register*

- *US Industrial Directory*

Another interesting resource is the *Index to How-To-Do-It Information* (Norman Lathrop Enterprises). This book covers approximately 55 magazines that feature how-to articles on everything from making your own plastic parts to forging your own steel.

For an excellent directory of merchants and manufacturers from around the world, review *Kelly's Manufacturers and Merchants Directory* (Kelly's Directories Ltd).

3.2 Patent publications

These publications are a tremendous resource when researching your patent possibilities, looking up trademarks, or scouting for a local patent attorney.

- *Annual Index of Patents, Attorneys and Agents Registered to Practice Before the US Patent and Trademark Office*

- *Attorneys and Agents Registered to Practice Before the US Patent and Trademark Office*

- *Classification Definitions Guide for the Preparation of Patent Drawings*

- *General Information Concerning Patents*

- *Index to the US Patent Classification*

- *Manual of Classification*

- *Manual of Patent Examining Procedures*

- *Official Gazette of the US Patent and Trademark Office*

3.3 Directories of corporate affiliations

The following directories list companies to contact if you are looking to license a product. The listings will give you information about the size and financial strength of prospective companies.

- *Dun & Bradstreet Million Dollar Directory*
- *Dun's Industrial Guide*
- *Standard & Poor Register of Corporations*
- *Standard Directory of Advertisers*
- *Trinet Establishment Database*

3.4 International directories

These directories will help you determine which companies to work with if you are interested in international licensing and marketing. In some cases developing a product for an overseas market is easier than developing for a local market.

- *Dun & Bradstreet Principal International Businesses*
- *International Directory of Corporate Affiliations*

Some foreign countries make great test markets for products that may require expensive testing and approvals in the United States. For example, fire protection products require Underwriters Laboratory approval in the United States in order to market, but in South American countries the same products do not require this expensive and time-consuming testing.

3.5 Directories for current information

This series of directories will give you up-to-the-minute data on financial and other aspects of companies throughout the world. This information can become useful when determining licensing strategies.

- *Business Index*
- *Business Periodicals Index*
- *Moody's Investor's Industry Review*
- *Oil Industry Comparative Appraisals*
- *Predicast F & S Index*
- *Standard & Poor's Industry Surveys*

- *The Wall Street Journal/Barron's Index*
- *US Industrial Outlook*

4. Information Databases

Many libraries maintain memberships to various Internet databases you can use in your research. Depending upon the detail of your research, these resources can sometimes save you hours of time at a reasonable cost. Membership costs thousands of dollars, but you can access the databases through the library's connection for a reasonable hourly charge. These database services provide more accurate and reliable information than what you might find generally on the Internet. Here are some of the most useful databases:

- **ABI/Inform**: General information on banking, finance, labor relations, and sales management. Also includes business and related journals.

- **Business Dateline:** Small business and business start-up information

- **CA Search**: Bibliographic information including patents, in chemical abstracts, from 1967 to the present

- **Claims/Citation:** Reference for over five million patent numbers cited in US patents since 1947

- **Claims/US Patent Abstract**: Coverage from 1950 to the present

- **Commerce Business Daily:** Up-to-date business analysis

- **F & S Index:** Domestic and international companies, products, and information on new products

- **Predicast:** Forecasts for products, industries, and demographics

- **PTS New Product Announcements**: Up-to-the minute new product releases

- **PTS Regional Business News:** Local press releases and general business reviews

- **Thomas New Industrial Products:** Product information and resources

- **Trade and Industry Index:** Resource for finding all companies within a certain industry

- **World Patents Index:** Access to information from more than 26.3 million patent documents

One database service that inventors can go to directly instead of using the library is Dialog Information Services — the biggest database service available. You can pay them to search updated information from their own database, which means you don't have to know how to do a search yourself. They can be contacted toll free at 1-800-334-2564.

Additional information can be obtained by using the county and city data books and the *Rand McNally Commercial Atlas and Marketing Guide* for regional buying incomes, retail sales information, and population centers.

While at the library, you can also check out the *Commerce Business Daily* for contacts in your area of interest, and *Tech Notes*, a government publication on new innovation.

5. Financial Support and Grant Information

For information on financial support, contact the following organizations:

- **Small Business Innovation Research (SBIR) Grant Program**

  Office of Innovation, Research and Technology
  US Small Business Administration
  1441 L Street, N.W.
  Washington, DC 20416

- **Venture Capital Exchange**

  Enterprise Development Center
  University of Tulsa
  600 South College
  Tulsa, OK 74104
  (918) 592-6000, ext. 3152

(**Note:** Also see chapter 6 on financing your invention.)

6. Inventors' Resources on the Internet

The Internet has opened up the world of research such that much valuable information is now available at your fingertips. Here are some useful resources:

- DaVinci Design Resources <www.uspatentinfo.com>
- Intellectual Property Owners <www.ipo.org>
- Invention Convention <www.inventionconvention.com>
- InventNet Forum <www.inventnet.com>
- Inventors Bookstore <www.inventorhelp.com>
- Inventor's Digest Online <www.inventorsdigest.com>
- Minnesota Inventors Congress <www.invent1.org>
- National Technology Transfer Center <www.nttc.edu>
- Patent Café <www.patentcafe.com>
- Patent it Yourself <www.patentityourself.com/>
- Patent Law Links <www.patentlawlinks.com>
- PTO Resources <www.uspto.gov/>
- Ronald Riley's Inventor Resources <www.inventored.org>
- United Inventors Association <www.uiausa.org>

7. Using Your Local University

If you are interested in an in-depth research project related to your idea or product, you may want to check out one of the small business institutes (SBIs), organized through the US Small Business Administration (SBA), found at almost 500 university and college campuses nationwide.

At each SBI, senior and graduate students in the school of business administration and faculty advisors provide onsite management counseling. Students are guided by the faculty advisors and SBA management assistance experts, and receive academic credits for their research work.

8. Industrial Application Centers

Industrial application centers serve as technology utilization resources nationwide for industrial firms, individuals, agencies, public and private organizations, faculty and student personnel, and institutions concerned with the promotion of economic and technological developments. The main purpose of these centers is to help users of new technology obtain information appropriate to their needs.

The centers administer transfer of technology — created in NASA development programs — through NASA's Technology Transfer Program. For a nominal fee, or sometimes at no cost, the centers will tie into the extensive NASA database, allowing you access to literally millions of documents from worldwide sources.

Hundreds of other databases can also be accessed for in-depth research studies. I have used the local centers several times to obtain reports for many of my projects, all of which were provided at no cost.

Industrial application centers are generally associated with universities, but they can also be located by contacting the Chamber of Commerce or your local library. You can obtain more information about these services by calling or writing the nearest industrial application center, which you can find by referring to the Appendix or CD.

9. Industrial Assessment Centers Program

This program, administered by the US Department of Energy, provides free, comprehensive assistance to small and mid-sized manufacturers. Teams of engineering faculty and students from universities throughout the country conduct energy audits or industrial assessments aimed at helping manufacturers improve productivity, reduce waste, and save energy. When their recommendations are followed, the results show an average annual savings of $55,000 for each manufacturer. The program's website provides an overview of its services, a list of centers, and self-help tools.

US DOE **Industrial Assessment Centers Program**
PO Box 3048
Merrifield, VA 22116
Tel: (202) 586-1298
<www.greenbiz.com/reference/>

10. Other Research Resources

Center for the Utilization of Federal Technology
National Technical Information Service
5285 Port Royal Road
Springfield, VT 22161

An important resource for new product development, NTIS is a central clearinghouse for the public sale of government-sponsored research and development, foreign technology, and market data. NTIS offers computer searches through bibliographic databases.

Clearinghouse for Federal Scientific and Technical Information
Springfield, VT 22151

This agency provides information on trends in specific industries, marketing data, new scientific technical reports, and new product information. When writing for information, request the Distribution Data Guide and Business Services Bulletins, which give information on products and services.

Department of Commerce
Washington, DC 20234

The Department of Commerce will send you information on business and defense services needing new products.

National Appropriate Technology Assistance Service
US Department of Energy
PO Box 2525
Butte, MT 59702

The US Department of Energy (DOE) can provide both information and technical assistance if you're researching alternative energy development.

Small Business Administration (SBA)
PO Box 30
Denver, CO 80201-0030
(800) 368-5855

4

Prototyping and Product Design

The ancient Greeks understood the ability of lenses to magnify objects, but it was not until the 1290s that Italian craftspeople discovered how to make glass clear enough to make glasses and telescopes.

1. Why Prototype?

An idea is just an idea until it takes tangible form. To lend credibility and value to your idea, you must have a prototype. A prototype adds value by identifying materials, tooling, fabrication technique, costs, and, in general, your invention's ability to be manufactured. But prototyping does more than just prove that the idea works. It also addresses your marketing and manufacturing questions and concerns. In other words, prototyping is a developmental stage that includes a critical evaluation function.

A product prototype will allow you to test the selected materials and manufacturing process you intend to use. It will generate key data concerning time requirements, processes, labor, and other unforeseen problems. Most importantly, it will turn that intangible idea into something tangible, a real product that others can hold and use.

My first prototype was a mock-up that I took pictures of to include in my business plan and to use with mock advertisements. As a marketing tool, it taught me a lot about pricing and features that were important to the consumer. By showing my prototype products to prospective customers, I learned information about my market quicker than if I had done the market research other ways. For example, I learned through my early prototypes that my products, when marketed correctly, could command four times the price than I originally thought.

The following information covers how to go about creating your own prototype, whether on your own or with help from others. Read on to learn the most effective way to prototype your idea or product.

2. Turning Your Idea into Reality

Building a prototype is often a challenging and time-consuming task that may require using other services such as machine shops, model shops, and fabricators. You may need help if you lack knowledge about the processes used or if you have difficulty obtaining materials. Regardless, if you want to sell your invention, you must be prepared to do whatever it takes to develop a prototype.

As you work on your prototype, you will likely discover that your product evolves throughout the process, changing as it becomes more tangible. You may make minor adjustments, such as switching the material from polypropylene to nylon, or you may make a major change, such as modifying the design to improve the manufacturing process.

Whatever the change, you need to be flexible and innovative in solving any problems that arise. Building the prototype is part of being an inventor, so don't worry if you're not an engineer, mechanic, designer, or model maker. You are the person best qualified to build your invention because you see it in your mind's eye and you know what you want. As the source of creativity that spawned the idea, you are also the one to take it into physical form — your prototype.

Your first prototype may be built of clay, wood, wire, or any usable material. Even the prototype of the car you drive was first made of clay so that the engineers could identify any design mistakes early on and make improvements. Use the experience of building your prototype to have some fun. Be creative in the ways you might build your invention. I once used my prototype knowledge to assist a local filmmaker in producing spaceships for explosion scenes. This knowledge was later used to create inexpensive vacuum-formed molds saving thousands of dollars.

Sometimes a prototype will need to be redesigned in order to utilize existing or readily available parts, so don't be discouraged if you find yourself going back to the drawing board many times. This is an essential part of the prototyping experience that often improves your invention, sometimes in surprising ways.

Once, while working on a Small Business Innovation Research (SBIR) project through the air force, I needed an inexpensive fire sprinkler nozzle for chemical dispersal. While the fire protection industry had the nozzles I needed, they cost $20 to $30. Because of my past research of other industries, I remembered that I could get plastic irrigation nozzles at the garden supply store that would do basically the same thing, and they cost only 30 cents each. Not only did I save money and provide better marketing potential, soon afterwards I developed a plastic nozzle for the fire protection industry.

3. Building Your Own Prototype

With the right information in hand, and with the tips offered here, you may find that you are able to build your own prototype, which I believe is one of the best aspects of inventing. You can be creative, have fun, and try as many variations as possible with the invention. No professional could possibly share the excitement and enthusiasm you will feel when building your own prototype.

Don't let industrial processes intimidate you. The libraries are full of how-to books on virtually every process known. Injection molding was once done with hydraulic jacks and plastic cooked in pots. Vacuum forming can be done at home using your stove, vacuum cleaner, and plaster of Paris. Molds for pouring lead, rubber, and plastic can be made out of auto-body putty. The tools exist to do almost anything if you're willing to seek them out.

I recently made a set of molds by using silicone adhesive. Using silicone to form around a part can offer you a mold for limited production. An inexpensive prototype tooling, you can buy silicone at the hardware store for about $2 a tube. Charcoal lighter fluid will thin most silicones, which can then be applied by brush. Reading different formula books from the library will give you other ideas as well.

One excellent book is *Ingenious Mechanisms for Designers and Inventors* (Industrial Press Inc.). Two other books that are useful for mechanical design are *Movements* (Lindsay Publications) and *998 Curious Mechanical Movements* (Lindsay Publications).

3.1 Your workshop

The place where you build your prototype may be the kitchen table, basement, or garage, or it may even be your whole house or apartment. Having a special place to work and think is vital to your creative process because it provides the necessary focus that fosters inspiration. Try putting an executive on a street corner to make that next big deal, and you'll understand the importance of environment.

An ideal work space will have a drawing board for sketching or drawing plans, a library of resource materials, and, of course, a work area for building your idea. Inventors' workshops are usually cluttered with scrap parts, hardware, and other odds and ends. I've found that most inventors rarely throw anything away. My workshop includes at least 20 years of accumulated gadgets, broken appliances, and whatchamacallits, which I treasure like the rare collection it is.

Why buy or build an item when you already have something in the garage that will work every bit as well? To an inventor, that old toaster is just the part for that new neutron heater. Sometimes, just looking at my gadgets will help me create something new.

3.2 Do-it-yourself shops

You can also learn a lot by visiting a local do-it-yourself shop, if there is one near you. Different types of clubs provide complete woodworking and machine shops for a monthly membership fee. These shops can often be found in the Yellow Pages under Woodworking or Hobby Clubs. Most are inexpensive to join and are a lucky find for any inventor.

Do-it-yourself shops provide you with the resources to build your prototype. They also offer expert help by exposing you to many other skilled people who use the facilities. Many inventors use these shops to begin production before committing to more permanent facilities.

4. Getting Help

If you decide that building your own prototype is not possible, you'll have to hire someone else to do it for you. Finding professional help in this area can sometimes be difficult because such people are not always listed in the Yellow Pages. The best way to find a professional to build a prototype for you is to look either for local manufacturers who work in related fields or for industrial model builders.

Another source of help may be the local schools, colleges, vocational/technical programs, and universities. Many schools require class projects and student assignments each year, and building your prototype may fit the bill. You will end up with a high-quality product that is either inexpensive or free. The disadvantage of this option is that it may take several months to complete your prototype. Remember that you have one year from completion of a working model of your invention to file a patent application.

If you decide to ask someone else to build your prototype, keep in mind that an unpaid builder could become a legal partner in your invention. It is good practice to have anyone who works on your invention sign a nondisclosure agreement and to get a receipt for all paid work they do to keep in your file.

5. Rapid Prototyping

Another option for prototyping that may be suitable for your invention is what is known as rapid prototyping, also called stereolithography. It is a process developed by 3D Systems Inc., in Valencia, California, that combines computer-aided design (CAD) with photocuring to build three-dimensional parts. Depending on the specific method used, the rapid prototyping machine constructs the parts layer by layer until a physical part of the CAD model is generated.

Although the process sounds like it belongs in the future, it shows how one product can assist in the building of another. The price of rapid prototyping has come down considerably over the last few years. This process is generally suited for products under 20 inches cubed, but some shops can do 24-inch x 24-inch pieces. A typical part 5 inches x 5 inches will cost between $200 and $400 to produce.

The operation employs photocurable polymers that change from liquid to solid in the presence of ultraviolet light. A helium-cadmium scanning laser, similar to those in CD players, supplies the radiation. A stainless steel vat that contains the photopolymer, and a "slice" computer, make up the rest of the stereolithography apparatus (SLA). Since no machining and no mold or tooling is required, rapid prototyping delivers physical representations of your complex designs in as little as one day.

The master SLA can also be used to produce RTV rubber molds and lends itself well to limited production runs. RTV rubber molds can produce as many as 1,000 parts if the design is simple enough. More detailed parts tend to destroy molds quicker. A typical mold can cost $500 to produce.

The best place to find rapid prototyping companies is to search the Internet, using the key words "rapid prototyping." Also, see the information on prototyping resources in the Appendix and on the CD.

Here are some of the rapid prototyping processes offered by these companies:

5.1 Stereolithography (SLA)

This process is the most widely used rapid prototyping technology available. A platform is lowered into the liquid resin (photopolymer) so that the top of the platform is one layer thickness below the surface of the resin. The laser beam then traces the boundaries and fills in a two-dimensional cross section of the model, solidifying the resin wherever it touches. Once a layer is complete, the platform drops the specified layer thickness and the next layer is built. This process continues until a complete 3D model is produced.

SLA prototypes are best for fast prototypes; often same-day services are available. SLA is a great way to test fit and form. SLA can be used for quick cast patterns for investment casting or for making master patterns for casting and molding. Additionally, SLA parts can be nickel or chrome plated or used to show quality parts via painting and texturing.

5.2 Selective laser sintering (SLS)

This technology uses a CO2 laser to sinter layers of powdered nylon directly from your 3D CAD data. A thin layer of powdered material is spread across the build chamber via a roller system. The laser then traces a two-dimensional cross section of the part sintering the material together. This process continues, layer-by-layer, until the 3D part is built. During the SLS process, the part is suspended in the powder so no supports are needed.

SLS prototypes are best for high-strength prototypes and functional prototypes, and can have snap fits and living hinges. They can even be used in high temperature applications such as wax patterns and direct metal parts.

5.3 Fused deposition modeling (FDM)

This is a solid-based rapid prototyping process that extrudes production-type materials, layer-by-layer, to build a 3D model. The build material is added to the FDM machine in a filament form contained in a canister. The FDM machine feeds the material up to a head that heats and melts the material and extrudes it onto a platform to create a two-dimensional cross section of the model. The material quickly solidifies, and the build platform drops where the next layer is extruded upon the first. This process continues until the 3D model is complete.

FDM prototypes are best for high-strength and functional prototypes. FDM processes can simulate ABS or polycarbonate materials.

5.4 Thermojet (TJ) or 3D printing

This process allows you to create 3D wax parts direct from your 3D CAD data. The wax patterns created can be used as concept models or as investment casting patterns. The Thermojet wax printer uses 0.001-inch layers to produce parts.

TJ wax prototypes are best for concept models and work well for artist or sculptor applications such as investment casting patterns.

5.5 RTV molding or cast urethanes

This process creates low-volume production parts from a polyurethane material via a temporary rubber tool. By using an SLA prototype as the master pattern, a RTV (rubber) tool is created. The SLA part is removed, then urethane is poured into the cavity of the tool to create multiple parts identical in shape but with production-like material properties. Since the tool is flexible, undercuts and difficult geometric forms are easily cast. RTV molding is ideal for marketing samples or where fewer than 100 plastic parts need to be created without the expense of an injection mold tool.

Cast urethanes are excellent for marketing samples for plastic parts as they are material correct samples of your product. Cast urethanes can be clear parts and can be produced in orders of between 10 and 100. Additionally, cast urethane parts can be produced in any color or texture needed.

5.6 Rapid metal castings

This process utilizes current rapid prototyping technologies to create either investment or plaster/rubber cast metal parts. The process required will be dictated partly by geometry and partly by material requirements. Investment castings are obtained via a wax or an SLA quick-cast pattern. Most alloys can be cast via the investment process (aluminum, stainless, bronze, etc.). With this process one pattern is needed per metal casting. Simulated die-casting uses an SLA master pattern to create a rubber/plaster tool. Multiple aluminum or zinc castings can be produced from a single tool.

Rapid metal castings are best for die-cast simulations or one-of-a-kind cast metal components. Rapid metal casting is also excellent for short-run metal casting orders.

6. The Design Process

Whether you decide to build your own prototype or hire someone else to do it, you need to consider the design process throughout. Prototyping your invention should serve as an evaluation process in developing a more efficient design — one that incorporates labor-saving steps and streamlined processes. With these improvements, your invention will become more suitable to manufacturing and marketing, and more valuable when it comes to negotiating a licensing contract. Removing unnecessary processes or steps early on reduces the cost, which later will add to your profits and sales success.

6.1 Industrial design

Simple industrial design principles must be applied when developing a product for the marketplace. Industrial design gives the product the outward form that expresses the qualities the potential customer wants.

Utilizing industrial design principles creates concepts and specifications that optimize function, value, appearance, and quality of products. True industrial design involves knowledge of many areas — including management, marketing, engineering, and manufacturing.

Each of these areas is important to the success of a product going into the marketplace. Other considerations that should motivate toward the right design include the company identity, advertising communications, packaging, and related activities.

The most esthetically appealing designs succeed more often than less attractive products. The automobile is a classic example of how design can influence sales. Even household products such as appliances have to compete on this level.

6.2 Design evaluation: Comprehensive design efficiency

It's important to see the big picture when thinking about prototypes and the design of your product. A design development process that is totally integrated has the greatest potential impact on your product's development. Manufacturing companies will see that your product can be produced with the minimal energy and labor input. For these reasons, product development designers and engineers have endeavored for decades to formalize effective developmental procedures.

Comprehensive design efficiency (CDE) describes a developmental procedure I developed in 1992 to offer the maximum potential for creating products that can be produced by the most energy-efficient means while still incorporating solid design principles. CDE offers a much greater variety of possibilities in product design and manufacturing processes than other programs such as design for manufacture and concurrent engineering, which include only small parts of the complete process.

CDE permits the conceptual design and choice of materials to be modified in response to the need for improved manufacturing efficiency and quality control.

This freedom offers innumerable possibilities for realizing improvements. When only a limited aspect of the complete process is available for modification, the potential is much more limited.

One example of poor design is a tail-light assembly on a car that requires replacing, at a cost of $100, whenever the $1 bulb burns out. The $100 may be reasonable for an assembly that requires mounting hardware, wiring, sockets, reflectors, bulbs, lenses, and frames, but the negative marketing reports to a consumer market could hurt sales. This is one reason why marketing considerations are included in the evaluation process in CDE.

Once the design is completed and the product produced, modifications, improvements, and redesign require far greater expenditure of manpower, time, and money, all of which contribute to potential loss of sales. Studies have shown that as much as 85 percent of the product cost can be locked in during the design phase. The lack of the knowledge of a more efficient manufacturing method can increase product cost beyond its competitive price range.

If you are not positive about why a certain process is used and cannot show a sound reason for its use, then you should consider improving your understanding of the design and what options may offer more efficient alternatives.

These same principles apply to parts count and assembly methods as well. Allowing the number of component design procedures to go unchecked may produce assemblies requiring many separate tools and manufacturing processes, increasing product cost and lowering quality.

Efficient product design is one of the most important tools for achieving ultimate success. An efficient design will increase quality because of fewer processing steps, adjustments, mating parts, tolerance accumulation problems, operator frustrations, material cost problems, and assembly fixtures. Using the best design will also reduce overhead costs and produce savings in numerous areas — cost accounting, direct labor administration, equipment depreciation, insurance, energy, engineering changes, production maintenance, material handling, quality control, inspection, purchasing, receiving, planning, documentation, distribution, and inventory.

6.3 Optimum design process

Optimum design can mean many things to the people working within different areas of production, some of which include:

- Evaluating and reducing manufacturing costs of a product during conceptual stages of product development

- Obtaining more efficient assembly procedures

- Anticipating future problems in manufacturing

- Simultaneous or concurrent engineering

- Improving quality by making the product simpler

- A communication tool (communications with manufacturing to understand problems and adjust accordingly)

- A procedure that considers production factors at the design stage

Here are several good reasons for using optimum design as the means for considering factors and variables:

- Optimum design improves product cost, reliability, productivity, and competitiveness. It also reduces inventory and paper work.

- After manufacturing starts on a product, there are substantial costs for improvements.

- Research shows that 70 percent to 80 percent of a product's cost is determined in the first 5 percent of its design life.

- Once the initial design is set, few people go back and develop a totally new concept; most changes are merely modifications.

- In many products, fasteners outnumber functional parts, representing a major portion of assembly time.

- Designing for productivity saves money which can be utilized toward marketing success (e.g., a screw may be an easy way to hold two assemblies together, but a snap-fit can eliminate screws and reduce assembly cost).

The first rule for achieving optimum design is to reduce the number of parts. Eliminating parts or reducing the number of different types of parts can have many benefits, including decreased material, assembly, and tool costs; improved product quality; reduction in overhead costs because of less documentation, smaller inventories, fewer suppliers, simplified production control, fewer inspections, and less rework.

Strive to eliminate adjustments. Design parts so that mating surfaces fall into place easily. Incorporate part functions; when functions are moved closer together, less linkage and fewer adjustments are required. When possible, use electronic correction as a substitute for mechanical alignment. Alignment features can be costly, but the added cost is usually offset by a reduction in assembly time. Parts that are not self-securing should be located immediately on assembly. Avoid the need for clamps. Ensure that parts are located before they are released. Use pilot point screws to avoid cross-threading problems.

Consider access and visibility for each operation. Restricted vision and access can make a simple operation a difficult one; always consider clearance for hands and tools. Parts that ordinarily are easy to assemble can present difficulties due to handling or separating them in bulk. To avoid handling difficulties, include features to prevent nesting (intertwining or locking together). To ensure non-tangling, always specify closed-end or compression coil springs. Include safe holding features for parts with sharp edges. Avoid parts such as E-clips and snap rings that require special tools.

Design parts to be easily installed. Eliminate situations where a part can be installed incorrectly. Provide some type of obstruction that will prohibit incorrect assembly and make parts symmetrical so that assembly orientation is not difficult. Use arrows or matching lines for quick alignment of parts that require orientation.

Maximize part symmetry. The more symmetrical a part is, the quicker it can be oriented during the handling phase of assembly. Parts to avoid are those with only a slight asymmetry. If the functional features cannot be made completely asymmetrical, a clearly visible non-functional feature should be added to define the orientation.

To test your product for optimum design, consider these guidelines:

- Test the need for each part's existence as a separate part. Is there a requirement during assembly or operation that demands separate materials or movement?

- Use integral locking features, such as captured washers to reduce assembly time.

- Move the functional components into proximity with one another to reduce connecting cables, linkages, wires, and so on.

- Use multi-functional parts if possible.

- Use off-the-shelf items only when they meet your exact requirements.

To analyze your design and identify features resulting in high assembly costs, follow these steps:

- Obtain the best information about the product or assembly. Useful items include engineering drawings, exploded three-dimensional views, an existing version of the product, or a prototype.

- Take the assembly apart (or imagine how this might be done).

- Reassemble the product one piece at a time, looking for problem areas.

If you have sufficient information to consider high production, become familiar with the high-speed or robotic tools available for your industry and include these considerations within the analysis.

In your analysis, consider whether parts are added one at a time during assembly. This would be the case for some assembly lines where workers add only one part at each station. However, for bench assembly and on many other assembly lines, the workers will often handle two parts simultaneously. Consider if the parts are presented in bulk and randomly oriented, or if they are available in magazines or special containers.

Performing this analysis provides useful information that will result in a reduction in parts and assembly time.

6.4 Designing for high-speed and robot assembly

If your design calls for high-speed or robot assembly, the most important and difficult consideration is the efficiency with which the individual parts can be handled automatically. The basis for cost comparisons will in many cases require expert redesign, yet for the production that warrants such changes, the cost savings will be considerable.

Here are some general rules to follow in high-speed automatic assembly:

- Ensure that parts can be easily separated from bulk and conveyed along the track of a vibratory or hopper feeder.

- Avoid parts that tangle, are flexible, have thin or tapered edges that can overlap, or are fragile, sticky or oily.

- Use parts that are easily oriented, such as symmetrical parts or those with projections, notches, or other orienting features.

Because the design requirements for automatic assembly require specialized knowledge, you will need to acquire this knowledge and/or consult with experts in the field.

6.5 Fasteners

The number of fasteners within your assembly can affect assembly time and reduce quality. The efficiency of fasteners can mean the difference between ten seconds of tightening screws or one second of snapping a part in place. There are many more options to the simple act of choosing a fastener than may be apparent. A standard screw in a standard hole may solve the immediate need, but a pilot point in a standard hole would be easier to assemble.

Because fasteners are available in virtually all materials, designs, and applications, it's important to know what you expect them to do. Only by understanding your options can you make educated decisions about an aspect of your design that might triple assembly time or cut it in half. Consider the following questions when choosing a fastener:

- Will the fastener be subjected to corrosive conditions?
- Will the fastener be used in high temperature?
- Is weight important?
- Should the material be non-magnetic?
- Will the fastener be subjected to high vibration?
- Does the fastener need good heat conductivity?
- Will the fastener be subject to cyclic fatigue stresses?
- Is the fastener used for electrical conductivity such as grounding?
- Is cost an important factor?
- Will the fastener be used repeatedly for service?
- Will the life of the fastener match the life of the assembly?
- In what industry will the fastener be used?

A fastener of a magnetic material should not be used next to a coil. A titanium fastener used with magnesium would cause galvanic corrosion, and a zinc- plated fastener should not be used with equipment that will come in contact with food. Fastener manufacturers will assist you in finding the proper solution to your fastener needs, but you must first determine if the fastener can be eliminated entirely.

6.6 Part symmetry

Using symmetrical parts will improve assembly time because they are easier to orient and will reduce your chances of incorrect assembly. If you have an assembly with a number of similar parts, standardizing the parts may also lead to symmetry. Symmetry in part design will reduce re-orientation; reduce part types and improve parts handling; and reduce assembly cost by requiring less thought.

6.7 Multi-functional parts

Using multi-functional parts can be as simple as using a shoulder bolt as a pivot, or using self-lubricating plastics instead of oiling a part. Multi-functional parts can also be as complex as incorporating sub-assemblies or parts for more efficiency.

6.8 Standardizing processes

A typical product assembly might require the separate processes of screw driving, gluing, and soldering. While each of these processes can be done quite easily, they all require separate tools, electricity, materials, labor, and skill. The same three methods of assembly could be done as well by crimping, with a change early in the design phase.

6.9 Eliminating or simplifying adjustments

To reduce weak links and improve the reliability and quality of your product, eliminate or simplify adjustments. Sometimes just moving parts together can reduce the use of linkage, cables, tubing, and wires. The more adjustments and related parts you eliminate, the higher the quality and more competitive you become because of reduced labor costs. Whenever possible, substitute electronic or electrical connections for mechanical ones.

One action to help eliminate adjustments is to include locating parts immediately upon assembly. The use of snaps or leads reduces the need for adjustments while tightening parts. When possible, avoid the use of clamps or jigs to ensure that parts are self-locating and self-securing in the assembly. Also use larger clearances whenever possible.

6.10 Nested assembly

Nested assembly methods use existing parts or a custom-designed base to implement parts using similar fasteners or locating means. A nested assembly will usually work from a central base and use one component to align another. Many times a nested assembly is performed in a top-down method utilizing gravity to assist in placement and locating parts.

6.11 Easy access and visibility

Obstructed access or vision will account for poor quality because of misaligned screws or parts not seated properly. If fasteners are required in a restricted area, consider snaps or other means, which locate and secure the part immediately upon contact. Poor access or vision will cause assembly worker frustration, increasing warranty repair and labor cost. Also, consider clearance for hands and tools. Restricted or inadequate access can make a simple operation difficult. Additionally, service is more expensive and frequent.

6.12 Parts handling

You want to know which parts are being presented to the assembly worker in bulk and randomly oriented. Early considerations for raw stock retrieval can improve your design by making the assembly easy. Labor costs increase with the use of open-ended springs as opposed to closed-end springs.

A captured washer or integrated washer on a bolt, screw, or nut can eliminate parts handling for that part altogether, as well as speed up assembly and improve efficiency. Parts with sharp edges can cause assembly workers to slow down. The same parts redesigned might include a means to grab the part, or rounded corners to reduce sharp edges.

6.13 Modular components

Modular components refer to sub-assemblies that can be snapped in and out for easy repair or replacement. Today's automakers use sub-assembly modular components to reduce service cost and improve assembly methods.

6.14 Improved orientation

You can further standardize processing surfaces by eliminating re-orientation. Build the assembly from only one side when possible. This requires less orientation and reduces assembly time.

6.15 Integrated efficiency features

Whenever possible, include features that assist in self-securing, self-locating, and self-aligning the part. Specification of any of these features in the design stage will save assembly cost and improve design efficiency.

6.16 Cost control process integration

One of the most cost-intensive ingredients in manufacturing is the labor. The most cost-effective design will minimize labor cost within the manufacturing processes required.

To ensure maximum cost and quality controls throughout the manufacturing activities, every element of energy and labor must be studied to determine how it can be reduced or eliminated by design-detailing modifications.

Most products can be manufactured from more than one material. The labor necessary with one material or process may be considerably reduced by choosing another material or process. The volume of a product an also dictate the required processes and material selection.

7. Selecting the Materials for Your Prototype

The selection of the materials with which to build your prototype can be technically demanding. There are hundreds of varieties of most materials, metal alloys, grades of steel or aluminum of the most commonly used metals.

The physical properties of materials could fill a library, but the consumer understands material selection in another way. For example, a fork can be made of plastic, steel or stainless steel, and perform the same function, yet the consumer's conditioning and bias will dictate against using plastic forks at a fancy dinner party.

Adequate information to support a material selection decision is available from most libraries. However, highly technical details as well as technical support and assistance can be obtained from almost all major materials producers.

When building your first prototype, you will most likely purchase the required material at the local hardware store or have it made at the local machine shop. Later, you will need to find industrial suppliers for larger quantities and also to avoid paying retail prices. Part of the prototyping process is finding future suppliers. Another benefit in dealing directly with the manufacturer is free samples. When was the last time a retail store offered you this?

8. The Manufacturing Process

To decide which fabrication process is most appropriate for your product, you must do some basic planning that provides the foundation for predicting economic requirements and production quantities. The volume to be produced is essential information before manufacturing processes and materials selection can be adequately evaluated.

The economic factors frequently dictate, to some degree, the materials and manufacturing process selection. If your new product is projected to sell in high volume, and an injection-molded plastic material has all the ideal physical properties, the choice might seem simple — until you find that tooling costs of the injection mold could range from $50,000 to $60,000.

The best source for obtaining information on where to locate appropriate manufacturers is your city or county library, usually in the business and technology department.

Manufacturers' directories available for your use include the *Thomas Register*, the *US Industrial Directory*, and *MacRae's Blue Book*. Some companies will only be listed in one of these directories.

A good starting point is the *Thomas Register*, consisting of several volumes listing detailed information about a company including address, phone numbers, product lines, and net sales per year. Additional sections include company catalogs and company profiles. This resource will not only help you find materials, but also potential licensees and competitors.

In addition, the public library has numerous directories for specific regions and industries. Many libraries now have these catalogs and directories on computer databases for keyword searching.

9. The Esthetics of Your Prototype

Esthetic function, when successfully addressed in the prototype and design process, will most certainly add value. Esthetics means "perceptive by feeling, or of beauty, or the science or philosophy, which deals with the beautiful." For example, think of a simple container meant to hold liquid. While any kind of container may be functionally adequate, the esthetic qualities of the design will make a difference to the success of the product. By adding value to the product, this has a positive influence on the sales against competing products with a less appealing appearance.

Consumers demand not only convenience in a product, but also that it be packaged attractively. Besides functionality, the features of form, color, and texture are important to consider in developing your idea, invention, or product.

The mechanics of a product require engineering and science, but designing the appearance is pure art.

Also, when choosing materials, keep in mind the way your product may be perceived. For example, consumers typically think of plastics as inexpensive, glass as breakable, aluminum or stainless steel as long lasting, steel as strong, fine-grained wood as expensive, and leather or silk as elegant.

10. Production Planning

You may have associated the term production planning with the function in large companies of ensuring that materials, resources, assembly labor, and equipment are available as needed. The fact is, smaller companies require planned production even more than larger ones, due to the vulnerability of smaller operations relying on sole-source suppliers. If your product depends on a certain part and that part becomes unavailable, what are your options?

Many times you will have to speculate on production needs. Your marketing plan will, of course, help in these matters, but consumer response will ultimately be the deciding factor.

Many new ventures use manual labor, based on the assumption that it is the least expensive form of labor, although in some cases this is not true. Poor production and the inability to respond to the demand of an increasing market can cost you both sales and profits.

Taking into account production volume, number of parts within the assembly, and most methods of assembly, the designer may discover that robot or special-purpose transfer assembly machines are best suited from the beginning.

If you're in a situation where limited production will likely soon become high production, high-speed automatic assembly would be a better investment in product competitiveness, even with amortization and higher initial product cost. Your situation may even require contract or private-label assembly until volumes reach the appropriate or desired level.

Deciding on the magic number in production requires an understanding of payback schedules and cost data. Finding the proper volumes for payback of automatic assembly, however, can make the difference in whether your product can remain competitive as volumes increase.

11. Building Your Prototype for Today's Market

To be sure your product is competitive, knowledge of competitive products, if any exist, is needed. Market information can be obtained from various governmental agencies and trade publications. Determining a retail price that is competitive and realistic will establish the basis for production cost, manufacturing processes, and material, and in some situations will affect the basic design concept.

No matter how inventive and clever your idea may be, it must be priced so that enough buyers can afford it in order for you to sell sufficient quantity to be a marketing success. Cost-effective development affects every aspect of the process. Throughout the product development process, you must be aware of how each phase of activity influences the others.

Much of what affects the costs of development are considerations of safety, product liability risk, feasibility studies, model making, and accelerated life testing. Because inventors usually build prototypes early in the development of their product, their thoughts are naturally directed at getting the idea or product to work. Most products are not initially designed for the considerations of manufacturing, including liability.

Industry has learned that a formalized step-by-step process to analyze a product promotes better design. Given this systematic approach to design, the inventor or designer of a new product can evaluate and analyze, within its design stages, a competitive product and one that meets all the standards necessary.

11.1 Consider product liability

Privity is a legal term meaning a direct relationship between two parties. When products have failed, causing harm, manufacturers have argued in the past that the product was distributed by a wholesaler or retailer, and that privity was absent.

In one landmark case, *MacPherson v. Buick Motor Co.*, the plaintiff was driving a new car when one of its wheels fell off, resulting in injury. Buick declared that the defective axle came from another manufacturer and therefore it had no liability. The judge, however, ruled that Buick was liable because of its responsibility to remove danger from the car. The newness of the car eliminated negligence in maintenance by the owner. The product must not only be safe while in use, but also during distribution and retirement (discarding).

Potential product liability risk can be designed out of a product by following these guidelines:

- Design to nationally recognized standards.

- Use components with statistical reliability.

- Use an accelerated aging test to uncover any defects and to dispute testimony of design defect in the case of product liability suits.

- Make a worst-case analysis of the product.

- Include notes to your drawings to eliminate hazards (e.g., remove burrs, plating notes, etc.). A drawing without notes determining a quality standard can lose a liability suit.

- Record product development history and design decision reasoning.

- Consider shipping vibration, which can weaken parts not designed for abnormal fatigue.

- Use warning labels where appropriate.

- Include proper instructions for use.

- Use independent testing whenever possible.

11.2 Product testing

Remember, the prototype phase of inventing is also an evaluation phase; an evolution takes place as your idea begins to take shape and gain that finished production look. As your product develops throughout the prototyping phase, take the time to step back, evaluate, and study your creation. This crucial stage in the product's development is the time to put your dreams to the test. If your invention can survive the prototyping process, it will have a far better chance of surviving the manufacturing and marketing stages. The success of your invention starts when you turn your idea into something tangible.

A convenient method for analyzing your design is to view the product in unassembled form or have a detailed drawing, preferably an exploded view of all assembly parts. In reviewing your design for efficiency, remember that the same creativity that fostered the original idea can now be put to use to improve your chances of success in the marketplace.

Ask the following questions about your product assembly as a test before the design is finalized, when improvements can still be incorporated easily and inexpensively. After using the best method available for evaluating the separate parts, proceed to answer these questions for each part. On the first review, you may wish to simply answer yes or no. Looking over your "yes" answers will give you a general indication of possible problem areas.

- Does the part move?
- Can mating part be incorporated in movement?
- Is the assembly made of multiple materials?
- Do mating parts consist of dissimilar materials?
- Does the part have to be serviced?
- Does the part have to be removed to be serviced?
- Will the part wear out before the product assembly?
- Can the part be combined with any other part in the assembly?
- Could slides, guides, or pins assist assembly?
- Can the part be made to be multi-functional?
- Is the part a fastener?
- Does the part perform as an accessory to any other part?
- Is the part a stock part?
- Could the part be relocated within the assembly to improve efficiency?

If you want to test your prototype for safety, contact:

Directory of Testing Laboratories
American Society for Testing and Materials
1916 Race Street
Philadelphia, PA 19103

The *ASTM* International Directory of Testing Laboratories is an online full-text search for services and locations of testing laboratories. The information on the types of tests performed, specific tests performed, materials analyzed, or other services offered has been provided by the laboratories. ASTM has not attempted to investigate, rate, endorse, approve or certify any laboratory. Each laboratory has paid ASTM a fee for their listing. Visit them online at <www.astm.org>.

11.3 Warranties

Warranties must also be considered when thinking about liability in today's market. There are two kinds of warranties: express and implied.

Express warranties are defined by the Uniform Commercial Code to be "any promise made by the seller that influenced the sale; and any description that influenced the sale, e.g., pictures, ads, brochures, etc."

Implied warranties communicate that because the product is for sale the manufacturer has made every effort to make sure it is safe and has at least the minimum qualities expected.

In 1975, Congress passed the Magnuson-Moss Warranty Act in an attempt to clarify the extent of any warranty given by a manufacturer. This led to the limited warranty, which limits compensation to the buyer.

If you are in the development stages when design may be changed in light of possible faults, the time and effort spent to fine-tune your product is well worth it. The responsibility of the design lies with the inventor as well as with the professional engineer.

11.4 Product life cycles

There are four life-cycle stages of a product:

- **Production:** From raw material to usable product
- **Distribution:** Transfer of the product to the consumer
- **Consumption:** The use of the product by the customer
- **Retirement:** The disposal of the product

Each of these stages requires consideration during the design of a new product. The production of raw materials can present liabilities to the production or assembly worker, which must be addressed. Even distribution carries a potential risk; if your product is improperly packaged and causes liability, you are responsible. One such case involved a longshoreman who fell through a void in a large cardboard package. Even though the man was walking on the packaging, the courts felt the distributor should have been prepared for such events.

11.5 Standards

Designing to established standards can be your best protection for reducing your product liability risk. The *Product Standards Index* (Pergamon Press) identifies many standard-writing organizations and lists standards that apply to various products.

Here are some important organizations to consider as sources:

- American National Standards Institute (ANSI): The main clearinghouse for standards.

- American Society for Testing and Materials (ASTM): Publishes more than 4,000 standards that identify test procedures and test equipment.

- Federal Trade Commission (FTC): Warns the public when a product is unsafe. Among its other actions, the FTC was involved in the removal of a certain type of imported doll from the market when it was found that the doll's eyes were actually poisonous seeds.

- Food and Drug Administration (FDA): Originated with the Food and Drug Act of 1906. Among many other products, cosmetics must conform to FDA standards.

- National Fire Protection Association (NFPA): Publishes all standards related to fire protection equipment. The National Electrical Code (NEC) is published under NFPA standards.

- National Safety Council (NSC): Devotes its efforts to accident prevention.

- Underwriters Laboratories (UL): Perhaps best known for the UL label, which is applied to products that pass rigorous testing, using one or more of its 350 standards. The UL label is well recognized as evidence of satisfactory design.

Other organizations dealing with standards include the Occupational Safety and Health Administration (OSHA), the Consumer Product Safety Commission, and the Environmental Protection Agency (EPA).

Groups involved in consumer products include Consumer Research of Washington, New Jersey, and Consumer Reports of Orangeburg, New York.

Terms Used in Prototype and Industrial Processing

Often, inventors are not knowledgeable of all the processes that exist in industry. The following list will help familiarize you with some processes available and terms you may hear when working on your prototype.

Antioch process casting: A variation of plaster casting using a 50 percent silica sand, 40 percent gypsum cement, 8 percent talc, and finished with sodium silcate, portland cement, and magnesium oxide.

Blow molding: A hollow extruded plastic tube is positioned so mold cavities close while air is forced into the tube, forcing plastic to take the shape of the mold. The blow molding process is used in making, among other things, two-liter soda bottles.

Carbon dioxide process: A green sand bonded with sodium silicate. Used to produce a very hard mold for fine detail; needs no baking.

Centrifugal casting: A molten metal is pored into a high-speed spinning mold, utilizing centrifugal force; a large pipe can be made this way.

Co-extrusion molding: The extrusion process (see "Extrusion molding") with material combination.

Continuous casting: Used for producing semi-finished shapes such as rounds, ovals, squares, rectangles, and plates. Done by continuously pouring the molten metal into a water-jacketed mold.

Core molding casting: A sand prepared with oil or grain to achieve finer detail.

de Lavaud process: A version of centrifugal casting in which water is used to cool the mold while in use.

Die casting: Inexpensive, fast, and accurate, but can only use nonferrous alloys because of their low melting temperatures.

Dry sand: A green sand that has been baked prior to use, thus providing a smoother surface finish.

Electric discharge machining (EDM): Machine operation that employs direct electrical current to "arc" away metal.

Extrusion molding: Continuous formation of tubes, pipes, and shapes of metal, plastic, and other suitable materials through the use of forming dies.

Floor and pit molding: Used for larger parts, which require being done on the floor or in pits.

High pressure laminating: Uses high heat and pressures to hold plastic to reinforcing materials that comprise the body of the finished product. Used for formed shapes that need reinforcing.

Hobbing: A ductile metal billet is placed within a hardened retainer ring to be plunged into a formed cavity.

Injection molding: The process of extruding molten material into mold cavities, allowing the hot material to form and cool. Normally used with plastic and powdered metals.

Insert molding: A process that combines dissimilar material within a part. A casting made from steel with a bronze bushing inserted is an example.

Investment casting: A metal casting process. A wax model of the part is prepared and imbedded in a special slurry of refractory. After the slurry has been poured, it is vacuumed to remove air bubbles. When the refractory has set up and dried, it is placed in a high-temperature oven and the material becomes fired, melting the wax and leaving a hollow void. Thereafter, molten metal is poured into the cavity remaining, sometimes by spin casting.

Lay-up: Plastic manufacturing process involving the use of an original pattern upon which a fiber cloth or mat like fiberglass, burlap, or sisal is combined with catalyzed polyester or epoxy liquid resin to form a hardened shape.

Loam molding: A variation of floor molding requiring a 50 percent mix of clay.

Machining: Employing milling machines, either vertical or horizontal, which cut away metal, drill holes, or slot and shape, tap threads, and otherwise sculpt solid material such as metal, plastic, or wood.

Permanent mold casting: Used for higher production runs, using molds made of metal or graphite, which are more costly.

Plaster casting: Used for aluminum or copper-based alloys. Produce excellent surfaces and accuracy.

Rotational molding: A process for making hollow parts, using a prepolymerized liquid plastic resin.

Sand casting: A metal-forming process. A cavity is formed by pressing a pattern into a bed of sand. Molten metal is poured into the cavity and cools to harden. Generally employed for rougher and sturdier parts such as manhole covers, machinery bases.

Spin casting: A metal-casting process in which molten metal is centrifuged into the mold cavities, rather than poured in. Used in making high-finish and accuracy parts.

Thermoforming/Vacuum forming: A sheet of plastic is heated and drawn or pressured down over a pattern to create a finished shape. Used for making covers and formed shapes. Plastics that can be thermoformed are acrylics, nylon, polyethylene, polystyrene or styrene, polyfluorocarbons, vinyls, polyvinylidene, ABS, acetal resin, polypropylene, and polycarbonates.

Transfer molding: Used for thermosetting plastics. The plastic is cured in a mold under heat and pressure. Usually used to facilitate the molding of intricate products with small, deep holes or numerous metal inserts.

Shaw process: Combines the advantages of the dimensional control of precision molds with the ease of production of conventional molding. The process uses a wood or metal pattern and a refractory bonded with ethyl silicate base.

Sheet metal working: Can include the forming, fabrication or use of blanking, part-off, or cut-off dies to form finished parts.

Shell molding: Also known as "C" process, used to produce a smooth finish by mixing sand with a synthetic resin binder. The loose sand is removed from the mold housing and cement is added to strengthen the mold.

Slush casting process: In this process, the cast metal is allowed to partially solidify next to the mold walls to produce a thin-walled hollow casting where the excess liquid metal is poured out of the permanent mold.

Solvent molding: Based on the fact that when a mold is immersed in a solution and withdrawn, or when it is filled with a liquid plastic and then emptied, a layer of plastic film adheres to the sides of the mold. Used for products like bathing caps.

5

Marketing:
The Key to It All

*Henry Ford's first car, called the Quadricycle, was
built in 1896, ten years after the Germans were
building gasoline-powered cars. However, in 1908
Ford's rugged and affordable model T surged
ahead. 15 million model T cars sold over the next
20 years due to improved production means.*

Once you have a prototype in hand, you are ready to begin marketing. This is a vital step if you are to experience success, and for those confident in their ability, knowledge, and determination, taking an invention to the market will be a great adventure.

In the previous chapters, we have touched upon marketing as it relates to evaluating your product's potential. Patents, trademarks, and copyrights all tie into marketing. Research helped you understand marketing, and marketing concerns drove the prototyping stage.

Now you are ready to dive into the biggest and most important challenge in either getting your product to market or getting it licensed, if that is your preference. (And for those who believe that

Think of your customer as buying an expectation of benefits.

licensing an invention doesn't require marketing, think about how much easier it will be to license a proven product over an unproven one.)

Maybe up to now you have been interested in making a better product or advancing technology. Maybe all you wanted to do was to get rich quick, but none of that will happen until you attract customers. Understanding and targeting your customer is what marketing is all about. If your product satisfies a need or desire and the price is right, your job is so much the easier.

Marketing begins with a product idea, but successful marketing is complete when the product is at the right place at the right time at the right price, with effective communication to potential customers.

To have the right product at the right time, you must identify consumer needs or wants, preferences, and motivation. You need to become familiar with competitive products and activities, economic conditions, and government regulations. You must develop an intimacy with the market, understanding potential customers and how they think and act. Only then can you target your customer. Think of your customer as buying an expectation of benefits. The buyer wants satisfaction from your product; your goal is to satisfy that desire.

This chapter discusses various ways of getting your product to market. Some products will require that you explore all these approaches; others will not. Read through them all to decide which method best applies to you. It's important to be creative and to try new ideas when you go about marketing.

1. Preliminary Market Testing

One of the most common problems facing new products is inadequate testing in the marketplace. Remember, it isn't what the inventor or manufacturer thinks about the product that counts, but what the consumer thinks. Your job is to make sure that your product gets noticed so the consumer has the opportunity to form an opinion.

The best way to test your product is to expose it to the public. You can perform a simple do-it-yourself test if you know or have access to at least 20 people, preferably as many as 50. These people should *not* be relatives or close friends, as they have to be objective and totally honest. This is the same kind of testing you did when you were surveying interest in your product (see chapter 1), but this time you will have your prototype in hand.

If your product allows for it, you can give away samples in return for people agreeing to answer questions about your product. If your product relates to a certain industry, try to get samples into the industry providing that they will allow endorsements to help in future sales.

This test is really quite simple. All you have to do is to show them your product and ask these basic questions:

- How much would you pay for this product?

- Would you buy it, if the price is comparable to that of the competition?

- What type of product are you using now, and why?

Start a file and store the data you obtain from these people until the testing is completed. Once you've collected data from at least 20 people, go over the information and see exactly how many said they would buy your product. If only one person out of 20 said yes, you have some serious problems, either with your marketing methods or with the product itself. In that case, it's time to re-evaluate your product.

Next, determine the power of your competitors by comparing notes on what product the people in your test group are currently using. Going up against a familiar product without having a unique feature people want or need could be considered marketing suicide.

Using your data, determine roughly how much people would pay for your product. To do this, average out the prices reported in response to how much they would pay for the product.

Now, if you really want to put your product to a good marketing test, calculate its profit potential. Take the average price someone would be willing to pay determined in your survey and subtract an initial 25 percent for the retail mark-up (if it's a specialty item or is sold in hardware stores, subtract 40 percent), then subtract 10 percent for the cost of transporting the product to the store,15 percent for advertising (if you intend to do any), 10 percent for warehousing, 5 percent for administration and your salary or miscellaneous cost, and 5 percent for insurance. Once all of these costs are subtracted from the average retail price, you will see what is left to produce the product. If the numbers look reasonable, your product has some profit potential. If the numbers are negative, you'll have to work to correct this.

The example below shows how this calculation works for a product that should sell at retail for $10, based on preliminary testing:

Retail price	$10.00
- (25 percent) Retail mark-up	<2.50>
	= $7.50
- (10 percent) Transportation	<1.00>
	= $6.50
- (15 percent) Advertising	<1.50>
	= $5.00
- (10 percent) Warehousing	<1.00>
	= $4.00
- (5 percent) Administration, Salary	<.50>
	= $3.50
- Insurance	<.50>
= Potential Profit	$3.00

(Note that if this product were a specialty item, the retail mark-up figure would be $4.00, and the potential profit would only be $1.50.)

Now that you've displayed your product and received a preliminary response, it's time to try test marketing.

2. Test Marketing

Test marketing is the sampling of a limited quantity of products in the test marketplace. In taking this step, you are experimenting to see what happens when the product is exposed to the real consumer. The results provide valuable information about sales potential, projected production needs, and potential profits — as well as preliminary data for determining how and where to market. Paying attention to and responding appropriately to this critique and evaluation will boost your product's chance of success.

To discover the consumer's reaction, you must first show him or her the product, and then listen to the response. The results of your market test will be very important and should be taken seriously. The data should be used to make refinements in both your product and marketing efforts.

For example, an individual purchased a $10 license to become a street vendor to test his new product, and spent weekends on street corners testing his idea. He made about $800 a day selling the product out of his van. At the same time, he set up displays in local stores. In the stores, his product netted about $20 a week. He is now doing what his market test suggested and travels from town to town selling his product from his van. You never know where your market may be unless you experiment.

There are several venues where you can try to test market your product. These include selling in a retail outlet, on local TV, on eBay, and at state fairs.

2.1 Retail outlets

In test marketing, sometimes you have to show some ambition and risk doing a little selling yourself. Anyone can sit at a flea market on the weekend, form a marketing study, and have some fun in the process. But if you aren't comfortable sitting on a street corner, a more conventional approach is to display your product in a local store, a competitive environment in which established distributors make their living. The challenge, of course, is to find a retailer who will agree to giving you some space.

In order to receive precious shelf space in the appropriate store, you will need to speak with either the store owner or manager to learn the requirements. This demands a professional approach. Don't just walk into a store with your product in hand and try to push it onto some shelf space. Instead, leave it in the car and personally approach the owner or manager. Introduce yourself and ask to set up an appointment to talk about a new product — your product. At the appointment, be ready to listen and learn, as a manager can provide a wealth of marketing information. Most managers have the authority to purchase directly from you and are usually willing to give a new product a chance, if it is properly packaged.

If you're going to sell your product from a store shelf or even a street corner, remember to use your imagination for unconventional and refreshing marketing angles. Continue to explore the test marketing data to determine what other directions you may also take.

2.2 Shopping channels

If you enjoy watching late-night TV and info-commercials, most likely you've come across QVC, or "quality, value, convenience," the TV version of an online catalog where people demo their products.

Many overnight successes started in QVC. This $3 billion business has a way of leveling the playing field for the right kind of products. Where most retail products rely on brand name recognition to sell products, QVC sells products with powerful demonstrations.

If you have a product you think would sell well on TV, this could be a shortcut to success. The categories on QVC include crafts, tools, personal care, lawn and garden, and fitness equipment. The products satisfy a real need at a value price and are easy to demonstrate and understand. The retail price of successful items is at least $15.

The bad news for some is that QVC will only consider products that are patented or pending approval since they are primarily looking to license and not produce. If this fits your situation, contact:

QVC **Product Works**
Studio Park, West Chester, PA 19380-4262
Tel: (610) 701-1120
Fax: (610) 701-8878
<www.qvc.com>

You can also check other TV shopping channels that may be available where you live. Your local cable company, or a search on the Internet for "home shopping channel," should direct you to what you're looking for.

2.3 eBay

If you have never explored eBay on the Internet, you should now. eBay is a way of selling your product over the Internet to a vast market. Every day millions of people purchase products on eBay, and it can become your marketing dream depending on your ability to produce the product.

eBay is a useful tool for evaluating new products, as it includes a way to determine how many viewers look at the product versus how many buy it. eBay can also supply you with more data than you can process on your own. And, depending on your situation, eBay may even assist in determining marketing feasibility.

If eBay works well for you, you might even consider setting up your own online store, which can be done for as little as $10 a month. Many companies now sell exclusively online and never bother setting up physical stores. Millions are made each day with online stores. Some even sell virtual products for virtual simulated worlds.

2.4 State fairs

Almost every large city has a state fair. The consumer at such an event is an entirely different breed than the typical consumer. Many people who would question, consider, and re-consider a product in a store will buy on impulse at a state fair. A booth to display your product can cost anywhere from $500 to $10,000, depending on location and city.

Many businesses supplement their regular business by selling at state fairs. Millions of dollars flow through the nation's fairs and profits are high. Of course, state fairs take place only once a year, but a two-week marketing campaign at the fair can be worth six months of consumer business to many companies.

3. Using Publicity for Test Marketing

Once your product is available to the public, enhance your chances of success through publicity. Publicity doesn't always mean prime time exposure or a television commercial. Actually, the best publicity for test marketing a product is free. There's an array of free advertisers out there just waiting to help you, if you know how to ask.

3.1 News releases

News releases are a great way to let the public know about your product. Simply contact the local newspaper and tell the reporter or editor that a local reader, inventor, or company is test marketing a new product. Normally, newspapers will not pass up a story of local interest.

The first article written about a business venture of my own produced more than a hundred clients. Newspapers offer a great venue to tell the world about what you're doing.

It isn't difficult to write a simple news release. You need a good headline, followed by the words "for immediate release." Include all your contact information, and then tell your story. Write about your product like a reporter would write a story in a newspaper. Write in third person and detail what might make your product newsworthy. List any particular person, event, service or products that may be of interest.

It is important to remember that the story has to be interesting and something that a newspaper or magazine would want to print. Try to emulate the headlines you see in the newspaper. Be sure to use the facts and stay away from the desire to advertise the product. Also, refrain from phrases such as "new," "unique," and "state of the art."

Here is an excerpt from a press release I have used in the past:

Tulsa Base for Sorensen Laboratories

Sorensen Laboratories, which makes and sells advanced chemicals for use in fire protection, burn treatment, and fire fighting, has selected Tulsa as its international headquarters. Dale Davis, spokesman for Quest International, said Quest has entered into international marketing agreements with Sorensen Laboratories, a foreign manufacturer, to produce and market the Fire Guardian, the world's first low-pressure automatic fire extinguisher made of plastics produced by Sorensen, using an advanced Halon chemical mixture.

If possible, you want to talk directly to a reporter. Asking what their personal interest in newspaper stories is can be very enlightening. Many reporters are always looking for new stories of local interest. I've been written up in the newspaper dozens of times, have been called on for follow-up information, and have even helped reporters develop stories and new angles to a story. Try to become their expert in the field, and you may find yourself getting to promote your product more often and for free.

3.2 Local TV and radio

Don't think that all TV and radio is out of reach. Call the local news stations and ask about the possibility of a news story about your new product. Many cable television stations will broadcast commercials for your product on a percentage basis, which includes production costs. Normally, products of interest to these stations are the higher-profit items that sell for less than $24. For air time and production of the commercial, expect to give away at least 50 percent of the profit.

Talk to local radio stations about using public service announcements or local community spots. Use every possibility to expose your product and yourself. Don't be shy. The publicity you create for yourself and your product will reach thousands of prospective customers, which in turn will mean greater profits.

A past associate of mine invented an innovative ring buoy. He discovered the importance of publicity when he found that people in Oklahoma, not having an ocean nearby, had little interest in his invention. So he devised a publicity stunt by renting a helicopter and jumping into the Arkansas River to be rescued by his new invention. He called the local television stations ahead of time and invited them to watch.

The publicity stunt worked so well that the local stations put the story on the Associated Press wire service and it was picked up by other stations across the country. Not only was the story seen nationwide, but he was invited to demonstrate his invention on a network TV show.

The prime time exposure he received would have cost him hundreds of thousands of dollars had he paid for the air time himself. Instead, his product was launched to its ultimate success when investors called from around the country wishing to invest in the product.

3.3 Magazines

Another publicity tool that can reach thousands of prospective customers is the magazine news release. To use this valuable tool, first write a good description of your product, listing all its features and benefits. Be sure and include your name, address, and phone number on the release. If you do not have a business phone, you may wish to hire an answering service and use its number. Some telephone answering services start at only $25 per month and can be a wise investment. Some services will also take orders.

In order to determine your best possibilities for a suitable magazine, go to the library and review *The Writers Market* or the *Standard Rate and Data Service Book*, which lists some 12,000 publications including all the magazines within your particular market or industry. Other good sources are *The Standard Periodical Directory* and *Ulrich's International Periodicals Directory*.

Check out the chapter on research for other publications (see chapter 3). No matter what your invention's category, there is probably a publication that covers it. For example, recently I found that *The Ballet News* is read by more than 30,000 people and that a magazine called *Bow and Arrow* has more than 100,000 readers each month.

To properly approach these magazines, prepare a press release kit consisting of a cover letter explaining that you would like to be listed in the magazine's new product section, a description of the new product including features and benefits, and a sharp 5" x 7" black-and-white or color photo. Always send your kit to the attention of the editorial department and indicate on the envelope that dated material is enclosed.

If you do not wish to hire a professional photographer, you can take the photo of your product yourself. Position your product in front of a white poster board backdrop. The best shots can be obtained by using natural light; a low F-stop setting on the camera will help obscure the background and draw attention to the product.

Keep in mind that some magazines require several months' lead-time, and some charge to list your product within their new product sections. You must determine if the price for that publicity is reasonable for the coverage you may obtain.

4. Pricing Your Product for the Market

Some products are so similar and competition so well entrenched that industry-pricing practices must be followed closely. Competition sets the price, and you, as a newcomer to the market, will generally want to sell at or below your competitor's prices. The strategy of making a better product and selling it for less than the competition is a good one only if the better product costs less to make.

There are three points to consider in pricing your product: demand, cost, and profit.

4.1 Demand

Demand orientation means prices are set by market forces. The inventor can influence demand through such things as product differences, services, and quality compared to competitive or substitute products.

Different product features and benefits can be offered to different market segments. Even with demand orientation, the consumer must perceive the value of the product to be higher than the price that must be paid for it.

4.2 Cost

Cost-oriented pricing is based on considerations within the company, including the mark-up above the cost to produce. Mark-up pricing is most widely used because of its simplicity and ease of understanding. It does not generally consider cost variations and the influence of demand for the product.

Mark-up pricing is generally used as a price limit, or a minimum price at which sales will be profitable. Many times a new market will start initial pricing by demand factors, sometimes referred to as "what the market will bear," later moving to mark-up pricing.

4.3 Profit

Profit-oriented pricing is based on price versus volume versus profit. Many times a break-even analysis is used to consider fixed cost, variable cost, sales volume, and resulting profits from sales in order to skim as much profit off the top as possible.

This type of pricing is also known as skimming the market. This is when a product is introduced at a high price to take advantage of the high profits available from customers willing to pay a higher price to be first to own the product.

After the cream of the market is taken, you then reduce the price to attract the mass market to the product and to meet new competition. The high profits obtained during the skimming phase will, of course, invite many competitors into the market.

One of the best examples of this type of marketing is the calculator business of the 1970s. My first calculator cost $69.95. Today that same calculator sells for about $1.

Two good books that will provide you with more information on marketing and pricing are *Pricing Practices and Strategies*, by Earl L. Bailey (The Conference Board, Inc.), and *Pricing Strategies*, by Alfred R. Ovenfeldt (AMACOM).

5. Packaging Your Product to Sell

The appearance of the packaging of your product can be just as important as the product itself. Think about it. The last time you were in a store, you no doubt noticed the hundreds of products along the aisles. On any crowded shelf, did a particular product grab your attention? If so, you were most likely attracted by the packaging. The quality or novelty of packaging is a key factor in marketing consumer goods.

Since packaging is the first impression a prospective customer gets of your product, visually you must project quality and confidence in the product. Appropriate packaging will effectively display your product in its best light to a targeted market. Consider that Procter & Gamble invested millions of dollars in packaging Pringles potato chips, a product that had more advertising about the package than the product itself.

Since packaging contributes so much to your product's chances of success, you should consider seeking professional assistance. Packaging designers and industrial designers can be located in the Yellow Pages and can contribute significantly to the market appeal of your product.

If you are not in a position to hire an expert in packaging, you may find it beneficial to visit the library for information on marketing trends and studies (usually in the research and technical section).

Your package must present a clean, efficient, and attractive way of getting the product from the manufacturer to the consumer. There are many kinds of packaging to choose from, and the product itself usually lends itself to a particular method and style.

Today's packages must not only be attractive, they must also be easy to load, resistant to damage, simple to pack and unpack for bulk shipment, and lightweight. They must also fit the retail space appropriately (e.g., Can your package be used as the display in the store? Will it deter shoplifters? Can it sit on a shelf as well as be hung on a peg?).

For further information on package design, read *The Silent Salesman: How to Develop Packaging that Sells*, by James Pilditch (Beckman Publishers).

6. Product Identity

Another important factor in the successful marketing and packaging of your product is the design and use of your company identity. For example, think about such names as the First Security National Bank, Great Northern Railroad, or Transcontinental Airlines. These names convey a powerful and imposing image, in the same way names like Bud's Hot Dog Stand, Whiz Bang Plumbers, or Frank's Bar and Grill imply a totally different feel, even though they may be appropriate for what they represent.

Your company name should be appropriate to your product line. It should be easy to read and, most importantly, easy to remember. An easily identifiable and attractive logo, brand name, or company name will add substantially to repeat sales and integrity, and will promote familiarity, confidence, and appeal in the product. When your logo or brand name is created, it's a good idea to file for trademark protection (see chapter 2). A trademark will give immediate protection for your logo or brand name and can be important for future licensing possibilities.

I highly recommend that you seek professional assistance to help design your packaging and logo; it will be well worth the costs. If that option is not possible, then at least take the time to study books on color selection for marketing appeal, design symmetry, style selection, and current marketing trends. Other study aids include clip-art books and printers' paste-up books.

It can also be enlightening to look at different logos and packaging layouts used for goods already on store shelves. Remember, most of these packages have cost the companies using them thousands of dollars to develop and test.

Here are a few good resources for ideas on trademarks, logos, and brand names:

- *Why Did They Name It?*, by Hannah Campbell (Fleet Press)
- *The Name Game: How to Name a Company or Product*, by Henri Charmasson (Dow Jones-Irwin)
- *Entrepreneurs: The Men and Women Behind Famous Brand Names and How They Made It*, by Joseph J. and Suzy Fucini (G.K. Hall)
- *The Company Image: Building Your Identity and Influence in the Marketplace*, by Elinor Selame (Wiley Press)

7. Marketing Through Meetings: The Cold Call

During the course of getting your product to the market you are going to have to meet with other people, either by phone or in person. The challenge comes in making that first call to set up a meeting, during which you must convince someone to spend time listening to you about your product.

7.1 Making contact

You first need to decide on the people you want to target. Who is the best person to meet with to get your idea to the market? It may be the store manager at a local retail outlet, or it may be the president of a large corporation.

Sometimes you will find that a phone call is all that is needed. Simply call the person on the phone and politely request a meeting at which you can discuss your new invention. That's all it takes — some of the time. But often, you will be turned down. Most of the people you will want to meet with are likely to be very busy and not willing to put aside time for such a meeting. In that case, you have to keep trying, perhaps working your way down the chain of command in the same corporation until you find someone who has the time to listen. That person may not be the decision maker, but if your idea is a good one, it will get to the appropriate person quickly.

When you call, if you don't immediately make contact with someone, always remember to leave a return phone number. Then, if you do not hear back in a few days, call again and leave another message. Remember that the busiest people usually have salespeople chasing them as well. Try to set yourself apart. You could, for example, leave in your message information that you are calling from your home or home office.

When you do connect with someone on the phone, you want to discuss your intentions in a professional manner. Rather that saying, for example, "I have a new invention and I want you to see it," say something like, "We have just completed market testing on a new product, and I'm sure your company would be interested in taking a look at it." Remember to be professional. Be polite, speak in a clear voice, and project the image that they will benefit from meeting with you.

If phoning doesn't give you results, you might try writing a letter requesting a meeting. This tactic can also be successful as long as you stay professional. Use your business letterhead and prepare the letter neatly following business standards. (If you don't have business letterhead, you may want to have some made up to give yourself more credibility.)

The key to setting up most meetings is persistence. Don't take it personally if you don't connect right away; just keep trying.

7.2 Face-to-face meetings

Ideally, you will be successful in setting up a face-to-face meeting. This is your best opportunity to impress upon a company that your product is something they need. But meetings can be intimidating, and you want to be well prepared so that you present the best image of both yourself and your product.

Remember first that a meeting is just two people talking. An advantage for you is that the topic is something you know a lot about. If your meeting is with more than one person, be sure to acknowledge everyone, but keep eye contact with whomever you are addressing at the time. Don't feel as though each answer has to be answered to the group.

A face-to-face meeting is your opportunity to shine. Talk with an easy manner, be truthful, and keep the conversation related to professional topics, and you will do well. Keep these tips in mind:

- Don't appear to be rushed. Never look at your watch.

- Do not drag the conversation on needlessly.

- Use gestures to communicate; they add visual interest and convey enthusiasm, which is contagious.

- Never go to a meeting empty-handed. If you can, take a sample of your product that you can demonstrate. Leave behind your advertising literature.

- Believe in yourself and in your product and you will be successful.

It is also very important to project a professional image, which includes your physical appearance and grooming. Like it or not, this factor can make a huge difference to your success. Some estimates say that people form 60 percent of their opinion of others by the initial image projected. Other studies have claimed that people who are well groomed are thought to be more intelligent and better educated. Here are some tips to help you make a good impression:

- The color of your clothing should balance and harmonize with your personal coloring. The sensitive use of color is a powerful business tool. You will look healthier and more attractive if you choose flattering colors.

- A darker suit with a neutral or contrasting shirt will help you look more authoritative. A medium or neutral color suit with a low contrast shirt will tend to make you look more friendly and approachable.

- Your hair should always be combed and trimmed neatly. A conservative hairstyle is always appropriate.

- Whatever you wear, make sure it's pressed.

- Never wear clothing with stains or that is dirty.

For women:

- Wear solid colors to give a look of authority.

- Hemlines at or below the knee are preferable for most positions.

- Avoid hosiery with patterns or textures that can be distracting.

- Keep shoes darker than skirt.

- Don't wear any jewelry that makes noise.

- Wear no more than one ring per hand.

For men:

- For a business environment, wear a conservative, darker suit. For industrial settings, wear dark or khaki slacks with a long-sleeved white or light blue shirt and tie.

- Wear a solid tie or one with a small pattern. The smaller the pattern, the more authority you'll project. The tip of your tie should barely touch the top of your belt buckle.

- Don't wear a sports coat with denim jeans.

- Shoes and other leather accessories should match.

- Wear dark or black shoes. No sneakers or loafer-style shoes.

- Never wear white socks.

Besides your apparel, you also must remember the power of body language. Social psychologist Albert Mehrabian found that the greatest part of a message is non-verbal. He found that 7 percent is content (what you have to say), 38 percent is the way you sound (the tone and pitch of your voice, accent, etc.), and 55 percent is non-verbal (your facial expressions, dress, grooming, and body language).

Keeping this in mind, you want to remember in any meeting to make your body and mouth say the same thing. Here are a few tips on body language:

- Know what your face says. Your eyes never lie, so why should your mouth?

- Try to keep 3 to 5 feet between you and others.

- The most powerful non-verbal cues are smiling and nodding.

- Stand tall and sit tall, you will look and feel more confident.

- Concentrate on listening.

- Control your reactive emotions.

- Avoid distracting non-verbal gestures such as toying with pencils, slouching in your chair, and playing with papers.

- Show acceptance. Even a nod of the head indicates you understand and want to hear more.

7.3 Phone meetings

If you can't arrange a face-to-face meeting, a phone meeting can work well too. Phone meetings have the advantage of often being more relaxing and easier, but they can also introduce some obstacles. A phone meeting takes away the personal touch, so it's even more important that you communicate clearly.

Here are some tips for presenting an effective, professional image on the phone:

- If your phone meeting is a scheduled one, be sure that you are available at the appropriate time and that you are the one to answer the phone. Have your meeting notes in front of you and be ready to answer questions. (Typically, a phone meeting precedes an in-person meeting, so be sure to take notes so that you can cover any missed topics in the next meeting.)

- If the phone meeting is unscheduled, and takes you by surprise, don't hesitate to politely interrupt so that you can move to a quieter phone or to have the time to turn off the TV or any other distractions.

- Learn from the pros. Telephone salespeople sometimes stand up when talking on the phone because it helps make them sound more alert.

- Keep a glass of water (not carbonated sodas) nearby in case your throat gets dry.

- Never put anything in your mouth while on the phone. That includes food, chewing gum, cigars and cigarettes, and pencils.

- Keep your pitch lower as it will help your voice project.

- It helps your tone if you smile when you speak. Remember, how you say it is sometimes more important than what you say. Your voice should reflect sincerity, pleasantness, and confidence.

- Watch your rate of speech. If you speak too rapidly, people start listening to how fast you're talking instead of what you are saying. Speaking too slowly can be irritating to the listener.

- If you ask questions, be sure they are easy to understand.

7.4 Active listening techniques for meetings

Learning to listen is just as important as learning to project your message if you want to be successful in meetings. Here are a few listening tips:

- Avoid responding too quickly while others are still speaking.

- Don't interrupt.

- Take notes.

- Paraphrase the speaker to ensure understanding.

- Avoid assumptions; ask for clarification if you don't understand.

- Concentrate. You listen and process information much faster than an individual can speak. Therefore, it is important that you concentrate on what the other person is saying and not let your mind wander.

- Allow for silence. This enables the other person to organize thoughts to fully answer your questions.

- Take the time to clarify details.

8. Trade Shows

Trade shows can be very effective marketing venues. There are more than 8,000 trade shows each year in the United States alone, catering to every industry from toys to automobiles. Booth space for various shows ranges from $50 to thousands of dollars for such mega-centers as the McCormick Center in Chicago.

Many success stories come from trade shows, such as the two women who spent $500 on a booth to promote slip-free socks at a children's-wear show and made $10,000 in one day. Another is the owner of Contemporary Designs, who wrote over $14,000 in orders in just one day at a boutique show in New York City.

Trade shows put thousands of potential customers in one place, willing and seeking to buy new products. Many new companies use trade show successes to finance their start-up costs as well as to support their marketing studies.

According to the Trade Show Bureau, nearly 85 percent of all trade show attendants have buying power, making trade shows a powerful selling strategy. Each month across the country, numerous trade shows take place, bringing together thousands of inventors, businesses, and buyers.

Before you attend a trade show, visit a professional display maker, if not to purchase, at least to look at a professionally made booth. Projecting a company image is essential at trade shows, and the impression you leave will stay with potential customers. But also remember that you may have no choice in where your booth is located. Many shows now assign booth locations by the lottery method, and you may find your booth at the front door or next to your biggest competitor with its high-tech, expensive booth making your little booth look even smaller.

One way to stay visible is to have some kind of advertising giveaway or gimmick. Small samples are always very effective whenever possible, but even if it's a printed key chain, use the opportunity to develop return customers. For further information on setting up exhibits, here are some publications worth reading:

- *Trade Shows and Exhibits*, by Donald G. Stewart (Association of National Advertisers)

- *Great Show Exhibits* (Designers and Producers Association)

For the most current information on what trade shows are available and when they are scheduled for, you can refer to your local library's business reference desk, your local chamber of commerce, or the Internet. For a comprehensive list, write away for the *Annual Directory of Trade and Industrial Shows*, available through *Successful Meeting Magazine*, or refer to the *Directory of North American Fairs, Festivals and Expositions*. Both are available at most larger libraries.

If you want to locate trade associations, look for these directories:

- *Directory of European Associations* (Gale Research Co.)
- *Encyclopedia of Associations* (Gale Research Co.): Lists more than 16,000 national and regional associations.
- *National Trade and Professional Associations of the United States* (Columbia Books, Inc.): Lists more than 4,300 national associations.

9. Selling to Department Stores

If you are thinking of marketing to large department stores, you must have a comprehensive business plan. The department store buyer will want to know who is going to manufacture your product, who your vendor is, and in what quantities you are going to make the product. Do you have a cost analysis available which details how much it takes to make the product, what the profits to the representative are, and how much your profit is? In general, you must be able to show, from beginning to end, each stage of the product. (See chapter 6 for information on preparing a business plan.)

Many department stores usually deal only with manufacturers or agents on their approved list. If you do not have proper representation or a manufacturer ready to produce your product, it will take longer to get in to see someone, if you get in at all.

If a department store accepts your product, you must be able to supply it with sizeable quantities in a short period of time.

Many new products fall in the housewares category, so if you do not have a vendor but one is required, you can obtain a list of manufacturers and vendors in your area. Write to:

National Housewares Manufacturers Association
1324 Merchandise Mart
Chicago, il 60654

10. Distribution

Of course, much of marketing is setting up an effective distribution system. You can get all the orders you dreamed about, but if you can't get your product to the customer, you can't succeed.

The methods used in moving your product from production to consumption are key external sources that can affect your pricing, sales volume, and success. There are three main types of distribution:

- **Direct marketing:** The manufacturer sells directly to the consumer through his or her own sales force.

- **One-level distribution:** A retailer, sales agent, or manufacturer sells directly to a retail outlet.

- **Two-level distribution:** The product moves through a wholesaler and then a retailer, or in industrial marketing, a sales agent and a wholesaler or distributor.

You may be wondering why a manufacturer would use so many middlemen, risking a loss of profits and control. Middlemen are used because of their efficiency and the increased distribution they give a product. Because of their experience, specialization, contacts, and scale of operation, they can distribute your product for less money than you could yourself.

Here are some important factors to consider in creating good distribution:

- Researching information for planning and facilitating exchange

- Promoting the product (distributors often provide this service)

- Contacting prospective buyers

- Matching your product to a buyer's requirements such as grading, assembling, packaging, financing

- Negotiating price and terms

- Distributing (the transportation and storage of the product)

- Financing (sometimes included by the distributor serving as an agent for collecting and dispersal of funds)

- Risk taking (also included because the product is out of your hands and has yet to be sold)

In evaluating which type of distribution is best for you, consider that when the number of customers is large and geographically dispersed, and when customers tend to buy in small quantities on a frequent basis, you should use long channels of distribution with many middlemen at each level.

Products that are bulky in relation to their value require channels that minimize the shipping distance and number of middlemen handling the product. Usually the best reason for using middlemen is to transfer some of these tasks:

- Transit of goods

- Advertising to inform and influence buyers

- Storage of inventory from which orders are filled

- Searching out and communicating with buyers

Selecting your middlemen is extremely important to the marketing function and should be done carefully. Your inventors' group may be able to help you locate a distributor, or you can look in the Yellow Pages under "manufacturer's agents" or "manufacturer's representatives." You can also use the Internet to search for local or international representatives. Finally, if you get to know store managers or purchasing agents, they may be able to recommend agents who work with your line of products.

11. Beware of Marketing Cons

In getting your product to the market you may be enticed by a number of companies promoting themselves as invention brokers or marketing experts. And marketing experts they are, collectively making as much as $500 million a year. Unfortunately, this money is made by preying on people who need marketing and development assistance.

These companies usually advertise in tabloids, on the radio or late-night television programs, and in magazines. Many have tried to stop these companies, but as long as there are people willing to pay, they are here to stay, providing phony marketing services that can cost up to $20,000.

Some of the warning signs to look for in spotting these marketing scams include offers of free evaluations, recommending further development while at the same time praising the product, refusal to work on commission, refusal to disclose other clients, and refusal to discuss the company or its background. Often they will imply that the patent office disclosure document program offers patent protection.

Once you've spotted a con marketing company, your best course of action is to simply stay away and warn others. Attempted legal action against any of these companies is totally worthless due to present laws on such matters.

It's unfortunate that some very creative people opt to pay someone to do what they can do better themselves and wind up losing their life savings.

12. Marketing Success Secrets

For increasing your chances of success, I can't emphasize enough the importance of understanding your market and acquiring all the knowledge you can about it.

The best and most inexpensive way to gain an edge in marketing is by reading as much material as possible on the subject. I've never read a marketing book I felt was a waste of time. There is always something to be learned by reading, but it's how you use it that is most important.

Here is a short list of marketing information available for your use:

Marketing Newsletters

New Product News
Dancer Fitzgerald Sample
405 Lexington Avenue
New York, NY 10174

International New Product Newsletter
6 St. James Avenue
Boston, MA 02116
(Selling to the Government)

General Services Administration
Federal Supply Service
1734 New York Avenue, NW
Washington, DC 20406
(Licensing Guidelines)

Licensing Industry Mechanizers Association
Suite 303E
200 Park Avenue
New York, NY 10166
(Mailing Lists)

Dunhill Marketing Guide to Mailing Lists
Dunhill International
444 Park Avenue South
New York, NY 10016
Compilers Plus, Inc.
466 Main Street
New Rochelle, NY 10801

America Business Information
5711 S. 86th Circle
PO Box 27347
Omaha, Nebraska 68127

Standard Rate & Data Service
3004 Glenview Road
Wilmette, IL 60091-9970

Magazines

Advertising Age
Crown Communication, Inc.
740 Rush Street
Chicago, IL 60611

Thomas Publications
1 Pennsylvania Plaza
New York, NY 10001

Resources for Direct-Mail Marketing

Mail Order Legal Manual
By Erwin J. Keup
Published by PSI Research/The Oasis Press
300 North Valley Drive
Grants Pass, OR 97526

How to Start and Operate a Mail Order Business
By Julian L. Simon
Published by McGraw-Hill

Direct Marketing: Strategy, Planning, Execution
By Edward L. Nash
Published by McGraw-Hill

Building a Mail Order Business:
A Complete Manual for Success
By William A. Cohen
Published by Wiley Press

13. Long-Term Marketing

Consider that half of the consumer products now on the shelves were not there five years ago. The average lifespan of a consumer product is only about five years, and if you do not improve your product, someone else will by producing a better one. Of the products currently available for consumer use, only 25 percent will survive more than five years.

One fact inventors often do not consider in the beginning is that when marketing slows down, so do profits. When starting out, consider the long-range plans that must accompany the excitement of seeing your product on the shelf. Remember, profits and only profits keep distributors, store owners, and manufacturers happy.

When marketing your product, be thinking of new ideas for improvements and derivative products. If you have already established a place in the market, use it to explore new products that may have the same potential. You may even be able to help another inventor get to the market. According to the latest marketing statistics, if your company only makes one product, you may have less than a 3 percent chance of success. Remember, marketing is finding out what people want and giving them more of it.

One excellent way of predicting future marketing trends is to read as many trade publications as possible. A company's success on the market may even be enhanced by updating its packaging to reflect new trends. For example, I worked with a company making an elaborate fishing-lure carrying case. After exploring the market, the company changed its focus to the medical industry. It did so after discovering that paramedics were in need of specialized carrying cases similar to the one the company was already making for the fishing industry. The medical industry was also an easier market to target.

Always remain flexible and listen to market demand. Your survival depends upon it.

6
Financing Your Invention

Although sailing ships were invented by ancient Egyptians in about 3200 BC, it would be 1807 before Robert Fulton's first steamboat made its maiden voyage up the Hudson River. The steamboat terrified local residents with its smoke, noise, and sparks.

1. The Need for a Business Plan

It has been said that a person without a plan is a person planning to fail. Your business plan is your blueprint for success — the document that will identify and quantify your business goals, objectives, and timeframe. And don't make the mistake of thinking you only need a business plan to talk to the bank or a venture capitalist. Even if you don't intend to make a lot of money, you still need a solid plan to guide you.

Creating a sound business plan requires an investment in both time and resources. A business plan is not just an array of information; it's a guide that has been thoroughly researched. It's your map to indicate where you're going and how you're going to get there.

There is no single format that you must follow in preparing your business plan.

In my experience, it's not how thick the business plan is, but what it says that's important. My business plan for my first product licensing was 28 pages and full of detailed graphs and charts. It paved the way for a $500,000 investment. But I have also licensed products with three-page business plans. How long your business plan is will partly depend on who the target reader is. On the one hand, it may be a local investor who may be familiar with your work and may require only a few pages. An investment banker, on the other hand, will be impressed with a more substantial and detailed business plan.

Before starting your business plan, you will need to clarify some points that you may have only vaguely considered up to now. Consider these questions:

- What exactly is your product?
- What are your goals?
- Have you given your product a fair evaluation?
- Who is helping you in your business?
- Do you really understand your market?
- How big and where is your market?
- How will you approach your market?
- How much do you intend to spend on advertising?
- What are you willing to do to stay in business?

Once you have honestly answered those questions, to the best of your ability, you're ready to start writing your business plan. There is no single format that you must follow in preparing your plan, but there is a standardized form that is typical of most successful plans, and you can add to or delete from that format as required.

Every business plan should contain at the least an executive summary, business history, product analysis, market analysis, analysis of the competition, marketing approach, manufacturing report, operation and management analysis, and financial projections.

The guidelines below will assist you in answering important questions and laying out your business plan. Even if a topic does not seem to fit your present needs, you should consider including it for future reference when your company begins to expand. Also, at the end of this chapter, a sample business plan is included for your reference.

1.1 Introduction

Write a paragraph or two as if you were explaining to a total stranger what your business does. Include the unique features of your product or company. Also, include a projection of the future of your business and a report on where your customers are now and where they'll be in the future.

1.2 Executive summary

The executive summary is where the serious sales pitch is located. It is where you describe the need for your product and business. The executive summary should be a two- to five-page overview designed to draw attention. If you are using the business plan to obtain financing, the executive summary will be the first thing a venture capitalist will read.

The executive summary should include a description of your product and business, target market, advantages over the competition, and who is running the business. Emphasize the special skills and experience of people in the organization. Provide a summary of financial projections for the next three to five years, where the capital to approach the market is coming from, and how it's going to be used.

1.3 Business history

The business history should include when the business was founded, its progress, a brief description of the founders, and the type of organization of the business (e.g., incorporation or partnership). State who makes decisions and why.

If yours is a new business with no history, describe your personal or professional background and experience as they relate to the business. If a prospective investor is your target, show why the new business has a chance of becoming successful.

1.4 Product analysis

In this section you need to explain precisely what the product is and why it is better than that of the competition. Explain how the product came to be and whether any other products are on the drawing board.

Detail all production stages and costs. Is the product difficult to make? Is a skilled labor force required? Do you intend to use contract labor or hire your own? Where are the suppliers located, and are there additional suppliers in your area, in the event your source goes out of business?

Explain in detail any patents, trademarks, or copyrights; packaging designs; research and development costs still outstanding; special equipment needed; and any pending or received approvals such as Underwriters' Laboratories (UL) or factory mutual (FM) label.

1.5 Marketing analysis

Provide a comprehensive description of your present market, if any, and any market research available. Include your forecast for sales and your intended sales approach. Define who your customers are, and outline a five-year buying pattern. How will you distribute to the market? What has been done to test the market? Are there any liabilities? Is the product guaranteed and what insurance is required to sell it?

The marketing section of your business plan should be detailed and researched; without a usable marketing plan, the potential of your business will appear weak. Provide information on channels of distribution, a sales compensation plan (who gets what percentage to ensure sales), your pricing strategy and its comparison with others, promotional concepts, advertising, and the cost of advertising. How do you intend to monitor the market and stay ahead of it?

1.6 Analysis of the competition

It's important to know what you're going up against. Have you researched the strengths and weaknesses of your competition? Include literature on competitors' ads in the business plan; use graphs or charts to show their weaknesses. Be realistic. Don't assume your new product can compete as well as you would like. Show that you have anticipated problems.

1.7 Manufacturing report

In this section, you need to describe the manufacturing process. Are you making the product or is someone else? Is it being privately labeled or "shopped out"? How is quality control guaranteed? What are future projections if sales rise? Describe your own experience in manufacturing.

1.8 Operation and management analysis

Here, list the directors, officers, and employees, if any, and include their resumes. Do you use any consultants, accountants, attorneys, or bankers? Include job descriptions of key personnel and compensation paid to each of these people. Include as many strong points as possible about the team and yourself.

1.9 Financial projections

Your financial projection is important to prospective investors because it indicates how much money you need and when you need it. It also tells investors when they will be paid back. At a minimum, you should include a balance sheet, profit and loss statement, expected source and application of funds, profit and loss projections, and a cash flow projection. If possible, include either five years of history or three to five years of projections. Obviously, the financial projections must tie to data included elsewhere in your business plan.

Additional information for an ideal business plan would include an evaluation of management experience and capability, an evaluation of the choice of business form, an outline of personnel policy, an outline of your record-keeping system, a review of the risk and your plans to cope with unexpected problems, and your pricing philosophy. You might also include your merchandising plan, credit policy, space layout plan, estimate of break-even sales based on profit projections, and even an opening-day balance sheet.

Your business plan will serve two important purposes. It will guide your actions, as well as those of your team, and it will persuade prospective investors that you have a concept that merits serious consideration.

With your business plan in hand, you are now ready to go out and seek funding from outside sources, whether that be your bank or another resource.

2. Starting Your Own Business as a Means of Financing

You may find it easier to finance your invention if you start your own business to support your idea. Going into business to manufacture and sell your invention is a major undertaking that involves more time, money, and energy than most people imagine. It is also very risky. Every new enterprise begins with optimism and enthusiasm, but less than 25 percent survive the first year. Many more go out of business the second year, and yet the few that do succeed and grow become an inspiration to future entrepreneurs. It takes dedication and diligence.

Starting and operating a business will involve, at the minimum, decisions on organizational options, management style, accounting techniques, marketing approach, legal and tax fundamentals, insurance planning, and many other considerations. Just filling out the tax forms can make many would-be business people reconsider. But if you view these matters as only part of the adventure, your dedication will generally pay off, and you may find that banks and other funders take you more seriously. And don't forget, all costs associated with your invention are tax deductible.

If you wish to start your own business, and promote and manufacture your own product, you should consider a business incubator. The small business incubator is an increasingly popular and innovative economic development tool to improve the success rate of new firms. An incubator is a building or group of buildings in which a number of new or growing businesses can locate and operate with much lower overhead cost than in a conventional space where rent would be much higher.

Incubator facilities are characterized by access to shared, centralized services such as clerical and administrative help, receiving and shipping facilities, conference rooms, computers, fax and copy machines, and assistance. Because the incubator is designed to promote the development of small businesses, it provides low-cost space, business counseling and training, and a co-op environment offering expertise and information to its tenants.

Many of the 200-plus incubator projects across the nation have been sponsored by private corporations interested in new product development and services. Many small companies starting out in an incubator get that extra edge to help them survive the first few years when mistakes can be all too costly.

3. Bank Loans

While most banks will not lend to new ventures, some are willing to lend money to small businesses to finance fixed assets, inventories, and accounts receivable where substantial collateral is available. Some banks even have venture capital subsidiaries that operate in essentially the same manner as private venture capital firms.

Bankers are a pretty conservative bunch who tend not to sway from the rules governing them. But they are reasonable when a solid proposal is put together. The way to a banker's heart is to speak their language. This means putting together a proposal that fits into the conventional categories.

The following are the basic categories that bankers use to classify loans, grouped according to the expected duration of the loan.

3.1 Short-term loans

Business runs on short-term loans. Technically, a short-term loan means less than a year, but in practice often expands to two or three years. Small companies usually seek short-term loans to finance receivables or inventory, especially in seasonal or perishable lines.

Short-term loans can be turned to many other purposes, from taking advantage of an inventory bargain to taking care of an emergency. Short-term loans come in many forms:

3.1a Line of credit

A line of credit consists of a specific sum marked off for a company to draw on, as needed over a prescribed period. The period may run only 30 days, or may stretch to two years.

Since repayment is tied to anticipated receipt, interest is computed only on the amount actually drawn, but a commitment fee of one percent or more of the total credit line is typically imposed to pay the bank for reserving funds that may not be used.

Some banks waive the fee in favor of a compensating balance or sum that must be kept on deposit. Other banks may work out a combination of compensating balances and commitment fees.

Lines of credit are popular because of their simplicity, but banks have developed several credit line arrangements that fit different borrowing needs. The cheapest is the non-binding line of credit, and may be your best buy if you're willing to risk the line's drying up. With no guarantees, your credit may be curtailed if your company's financial position deteriorates, or even if your industry seems headed for hard times.

3.1b   Inventory loans

When a small company with seasonal borrowing needs comes in for a loan of $25,000 to $200,000, some banks shy away from the formal line of credit, preferring to write what they call short-term loans to carry inventory. This is where the collateral is the inventory itself.

Floor planning is a term for an arrangement used by bit ticket retailers where loans are collateralized by specific inventory items. The usual inventory loan runs six to nine months and requires the same 30-day annual clean-up as a line of credit, if you want an extension.

3.1c   Commercial loans

Some big banks funnel much of their short-term lending into commercial, or Time loans, which minimize bookkeeping for both the lender and the borrower. Requiring no installments, a commercial loan is simply repaid in a lump sum at the end of the term, typically three to six months.

3.1d   Accounts receivable financing

Small companies in almost every industry today find that receivables are tying up inordinate amounts of working capital, so they're turning to their banks for loans that will convert unpaid accounts into cash for working capital.

One limitation on receivables financing that doesn't apply to other short-term loans is that most banks set minimums based on the cost of monitoring such loans.

3.1e Factoring

One of the oldest methods of commercial lending is factoring, a variation of accounts receivable financing in which the bank buys receivables outright. There are some limits to factoring. The bank subjects receivables to rigid scrutiny before making any purchases, to screen out the poorest risks.

3.2 Medium-term loans

Medium-term loans are typically one-to-five year loans and may be used for financing machinery and equipment, including furniture and fixtures, plant alteration, and expansion. However, many times banks will ask for additional collateral on medium-term loans.

There are two kinds of medium-term loans: the term loan and the monthly payment business loan.

3.2a Term loan

Most term loans providing 80 percent to 90 percent of the total costs are written either for five years, with a refinancing clause, or for the useful life of the asset. The typical repayment schedule calls for quarterly installment of principal plus interest.

Principal payments will remain constant, but the interest computed on the outstanding amount declines over the term of the loan.

3.2b Monthly payment business loan

A business loan with quarterly installments is a variation of the term loan. The payments are set up as equal monthly payments throughout the loan period.

3.3 Long-term loans

Long-term loans are loans of five or more years and are the hardest to get approved for. They are often used for major expansions or the purchase of real property and fall into several categories.

3.3a   Commercial and industrial mortgages

Commercial and industrial mortgages may be written in a variety of ways, depending on the value of the building, your company's long-range profit projections, and the bank's lending policies. This can be similar to a standard 25-year home loan.

3.3b   Real estate loans

For companies that already own property, real estate loans offer a way to pay less interest and to refinance their real estate in order to obtain working or inventory capital.

3.3c   Personal loans

Many bankers believe an owner's personal assets should provide much of the financing for working capital, so you may have to consider a secured personal loan in your long-term financing plans. Any property in your own name can be used as collateral.

3.3d   Asset-based loans

Typically used by large corporations, this type of loan is appropriate for leveraged buy-outs, in which the target company's own assets are used to finance the takeover. Assets can include raw materials, inventory, machinery, and equipment.

3.3e   Start-up loans

When funds are raised by personal loans, you may additionally be able to gain start-up loans that are guaranteed through the Small Business Administration (SBA). This procedure requires a lot of paperwork but can be worthwhile for the start-up operation. It's best to work with a bank that participates in the SBA's Certification Program.

4. The Loan Proposal

Every banker wants to hear how their loan will improve your company. The loan proposal should speak to this question. It should offer insight into your business venture and detail your knowledge of the industry. Bankers need to trust your knowledge and skills within the industry.

A loan proposal is in many ways similar to a business plan. Some banks will ask for your business plan, but others will want to see a specific loan proposal. However, you can certainly use the information from your business plan to create your loan proposal.

These are the different parts of a loan proposal:

- **Summary:** Typically the general information on the first page. It consists of your company name and address, the nature of your business, the amount sought, the purpose of the loan, and the source of repayment.

- **Top management profiles:** Typically a paragraph or two on the key players within your organization. This may also include consultants and other support organizations. It's important to remember that bankers see security in an experienced management leading a company.

- **Business description:** A detailed description of what your business does and why it is successful in the industry. Describe any inventory, equipment, or other assets. Bankers tend to favor established markets and conventional merchandise.

- **Projections:** Your predicted share of the market and your growth opportunities. Bankers like to see account receivables with less than 60-day payments and that are spread out among a large customer base. Talk about your one- to five-year projections for market share.

- **Financial statements:** If possible, balance sheets and income statements for the last three years. Remember that past and current statements must be exact. These statements will most likely be audited. Bankers will typically match your financial projects with general industry standards, so make your goals reasonable.

- **Purpose:** Details of your proposed use of the loan. Make this section as detailed as possible and account for working capital during this time if the loan is not for working capital.

- **Amount:** The specific amount and the reason you need it. Use past experience of past figures to help explain where this amount comes from. Don't ask for more than you need to spend. Loan proposals are typically not a back and forth negotiation.

- **Repayment plan:** The most important part to any banker. Detail how you expect to repay the loan. If the loan is for an asset such as equipment, the loan must be paid back during the useful life of the equipment.

Many people assume that their own personal bank is the best suited to work with due to their support through the years. I've personally found this not to be true. I was surprised to discover that my bank turned down a loan request. I had been a member for some 20 plus years and always had great credit. It turned out, however, that they used a credit reporting service that had incorrect information on a past account.

I went to another lender and received the loan I needed with ease. Then I pulled all my funds from my bank and placed them elsewhere where I received more service and even more interest on my money. So in the end, it turned out that the denial for the loan was beneficial for me.

5. Other Funding Sources

There are various other sources from which to obtain capital. While each has its benefits and drawbacks, it's often your particular situation that determines where you will look for start-up money or investment capital. Here is an overview of each of the different means available:

5.1 Family, friends, and savings

In the early stages of development, it may be easier or more expedient to obtain financial assistance from family or friends. Personal savings are also frequently used to get started. Later, an investor may take a favorable view of your project.

Always remember, though, that with any investment comes risk, and that nothing can turn close relationships sour faster than being in debt. So be extra cautious if you choose to borrow from family and friends.

5.2 Government lending programs

The Small Business Administration (SBA) provides financing to small business through direct loans or loan guarantees made to private lending institutions. To obtain a list of your local banks that are approved SBA centers, visit the library or consult your telephone directory for the phone number of the SBA office in your area.

5.3 Government grant programs

One good way to receive funds for new idea development is when the idea also serves a need for the government. Through the SBA, Office of Innovation, Research and Technology, you can receive SBIR Pre-Solicitation Announcements. If you qualify as a small business, you can receive grants for research and development through the US Department of Defense, Department of Commerce, Department of Energy, Department of Health and Human Services, or the Environmental Protection Agency.

The three-phase program grants up to $75,000 in the first phase, up to $800,000 in the second phase, and phase three is conducted by nonfederal funds to take the solution to commercial applications.

For further information and to be included on the government's mailing list, visit the website of the Office of Innovation, Research and Technology, US Small Business Administration, at <www.sbaonline.sba.gov/sbir/>.

This website is the central source available for researching all US Small Business Administration (SBA) programs and all Small Business Innovation Research (SBIR) grants. It will lead you to information on the numerous programs available today to help inventors and small businesses. Since the website is continually updated, visit it often for the latest available information.

5.4 Private or exempt public offerings

While an unlikely source for immediate start-up capital, a company in an expansion phase may be able to raise capital for promoting new products without fully registering its offering with the Securities and Exchange Commission (SEC) or similar state commissions. One should consider such factors as lag time between initiation and actual financing, and the complexities of having private shareholders.

5.5 Registered public offerings

A full-scale registration with the SEC and state authorities may be required when seeking larger amounts of capital. As with private placements, most small ventures will not view public offerings as an attractive financing source due to the time, cost, and registration requirements involved.

5.6 Venture capitalists

Venture capital firms are usually privately owned or formed as general or limited partnerships, and they are composed primarily of institutional investors or wealthy individuals. Most venture capital firms seek investments in which they expect to realize a high rate of return — often 10 to 1 or higher.

Here are some sources for finding venture capital:

National Venture Capital Association (NVCA)

National Association of Small Business Investment Companies (NASBIC)

Department of Commerce

National Science Foundation (NSF) <www.nsf.gov>

Whatever source of funding you choose will depend largely on your own situation and knowledge or background. One consideration that may be overlooked, however, is the importance of understanding your state and federal securities laws on fundraising efforts. For example, when borrowing from friends and relatives, an inventor may forget that any efforts to raise capital require compliance with state and federal securities laws. Check with your legal adviser.

SAMPLE 1
Business Plan

Executive Summary

(*Company Name*) will be formed as a marketing company specializing in the marketing of a new service (or product) in the local and international marketplace. Its founders are the inventors of the service (or product) and marketers of products and services. They are founding (*Your Company Name*) to formalize the new service (or product) marketing services.

Mission

(**Your Company Name**) offers the market a reliable, high-quality alternative to the other services (or products) on the market today. A true alternative to (*list the competition*) that offers the very best in this (*list your market*) market. Consumers will soon know that purchasing (*Your Company Product*) is a smarter way to solve their needs. (*List the service or product's advantage here.*) (*Your Company Name*) must also be able to maintain a financial balance, charging a fair value for its services (or products), and delivering an even higher value to the end user. Initial focus will be the development of local markets in the United States and later developing the European market.

Key to Success

List your product or service advantages here.

Company Summary

(**Your Company Name**) is a new company providing a high-level of expertise in business and product development with excellent distribution strategies and innovative marketing of new products. It will focus initially on providing two kinds of international triangles:

Providing United States clients with development for European and Latin American markets.

Providing European clients with development for the United States and Latin American markets.

As the company grows it will take on people to grow and develop new markets in related markets, such as the rest of Latin America, the Far East, and similar markets. As it grows it will also look for additional leverage by taking other new related products to the marketplace.

Company Ownership

(**Your Company Name**) will be created as an Incorporation based in (*Your City*), owned by its principal investors and principal operators. As of this writing it has not been chartered yet and is still considering alternatives of legal formation.

SAMPLE 1 — Continued

Start-up Summary

Total start-up expense (including legal costs, logo design, stationery, and related expenses) comes to (List $ amount here). Start-up assets required include (List $) in short-term assets (office furniture, etc.) and (List $) in initial cash to handle the first few months of consulting operations as sales and accounts receivable play through the cash flow. The details are included in the table.

Start-up expenses

Legal	$
Stationery, etc.	$
Brochures	$
Consultants	$
Insurance	$
Expensed equipment	$
Other	$
Total start-up expense	$

Start-up assets needed

Cash requirements	$
Start-up inventory	$
Other short-term assets	$
Total short-term assets	$
Long-term assets	$
Capital assets	$
Total assets	$
Total start-up requirements	$
Left to finance	$

Start-up funding plan

Investment

Investor 1	$
Investor 2	$
Other	$
Total investment	$

SAMPLE 1 — Continued

Short-term borrowing

Unpaid expenses	$
Short-term loans	$
Interest-free short-term loans	$
Subtotal short-term borrowing	$
Long-term borrowing	$
Total borrowing	$
Loss at start-up	$
Total equity	$
Total debt and equity	$

Company Services
(*Your Company Name*) offers expertise in distribution, development, and market development. Test markets have been performed and products sold and packaged in various ways that allow clients to choose the best products. Sales and market representation are in place with existing companies interested in selling our product.

Company Locations and Facilities
The initial office will be established in a quality office space in (*Your Town and State*) in the heart of the US market.

Services and Products
(*Your Company Name*) offers the expertise of a marketing and development company to develop new product distribution and new market segments in new markets.

(Examples are:)

Service and Product Description

New Product Development

Consulting

Project Consulting

Market Research

SAMPLE 1 — Continued

Competitive Comparison
(List all competitors that you are aware of)

Main Competitors
(List specific products and/or services)

Sales Literature
The business will begin with a general brochure introducing the product to the retail industry. This material will be developed as part of the start-up expenses. Literature and mailings for the initial market forums will be very important, with the need to establish a high-quality look and feel for our product.

Future Services and Products
In the future (*Your Company Name*) will broaden the coverage by expanding into additional markets and additional product areas.

Market Analysis Summary

(*Your Company Name*) will be focusing on marketing our new product into markets in the United States. After this market is established, we will develop European and Latin American markets. Our target market is (*list your desired market*).

Industry Analysis
(List any reports or studies you have obtained from the resources you use)

Industry Participants
(List any partnerships and organizations that you have worked with)

Distribution Patterns
(List how you are going to get the product to the marketplace)

Trucking
Rail
Fed-Ex
UPS
Mail

Competition and Buying Patterns
(List special events that may cause sales to rise, i.e., Christmas sales or other events)

SAMPLE 1 — Continued

Strategy Summary
(Your Company Name) will focus on three geographical markets: the United States, Europe, and Latin America. The target customer is usually a manager in a larger corporation, and occasionally an owner or president of a medium-sized corporation in a high-growth market.

Pricing Strategy
(Your Company Name) will be priced at the upper edge of what the market will bear, competing with the name brand products. The pricing fits with the general positioning of the market. Market research reports should be priced at $ per product, which will of course require that product be well presented.

Sales Forecast
The sales forecast monthly summary is included in the appendix. The annual sales projections are included in the following table.

Sales	2005	2006	2007
Retainer Consulting	$	$	$
Project Consulting	$	$	$
Market Research	$	$	$
Strategic Reports	$	$	$
Other	$	$	$
Total Sales	$	$	$

Cost of sales	2005	2006	2007
Retainer Consulting	$	$	$
Project Consulting	$	$	$
Market Research	$	$	$
Strategic Reports	$	$	$
Other	$	$	$
Total Cost of Sales	$	$	$

Strategic Alliance
At this writing, strategic alliances with (*List Companies*) are possibilities, based on the content of existing discussions. Given the background of prospective partners, we might also be talking to European companies including (List Companies) and others, and to US companies related to ABC Company. In Latin America we would be looking at the key local similar product vendor.

SAMPLE 1 — Continued

Management Summary
The initial management team depends on the founders themselves, with little backup. As we grow we will take on additional consulting help, plus graphic/editorial, sales, and marketing.

Organizational Structure
(*Your Company Name*) should be managed by working partners, and in the beginning we assume three to five partners:

   (*List any partners*)

Management Team
(*Your Company Name*) business requires a very high level of international experience and expertise. This means that it will not be easy to leverage in the common marketing company mode in which partners run the business and make sales, while associates fulfill. Partners will necessarily be involved in the fulfillment of the core business proposition, providing the expertise to the clients.

   The initial personnel plan is still tentative. It should involve three to five partners, one to three consultants, one strong editorial/graphic person with good staff support, one strong marketing person, an office manager, and a secretary. Later we will add more partners, consultants, and sales staff.

   Founders' resumes are included as an additional attachment to this plan.

Personnel Plan
(*List projected staffing needs*)

Financial Plan
We will maintain a conservative financial strategy, based on developing capital for future growth.

Important Assumptions
(*List any assumptions that may be relevant*)

Key Financial Indicators

Sales
Gross Margin
Operating Expense
Collection

SAMPLE 1 — Continued

Break-Even Analysis
(*List at what point the company will be profitable. Charts and tables can be useful here.*)

Projected Profit and Loss
The detailed monthly pro-forma income statement for the first year is included in the appendixes. The annual estimates are included here.

(This is an example of a Pro-forma Income Statement)

	2005	2006	2007
Sales	$	$	$
Cost of Sales	$	$	$
Other	$	$	$
Total Cost of Sales	$	$	$
Gross margin	$	$	$
Gross margin percent	%	%	%
Operating expenses			
Advertising/Promotion	$	$	$
Public Relations	$	$	$
Travel	$	$	$
Miscellaneous	$	$	$
Payroll expense	$	$	$
Leased Equipment	$	$	$
Utilities	$	$	$
Insurance	$	$	$
Depreciation	$	$	$
Rent	$	$	$
Payroll Burden	$	$	$
Contract/Consultants	$	$	$
Other	$	$	$
Total Operating Expenses	$	$	$

SAMPLE 1 — Continued

Profit before Interest and Taxes	$	$	$
Interest Expense ST	$	$	$
Interest Expense LT	$	$	$
Taxes Incurred	$	$	$
Net Profit	$	$	$
Net Profit/Sales	%	%	%
Projected Cash Flow	$	$	$

Cash flow projections are critical to our success. The monthly cash flow is shown in the illustration, with one bar representing the cash flow per month and the other the monthly balance. The annual cash flow figures are included here. Detailed monthly numbers are included in the appendixes.

Appendixes
(*The Appendixes in a Business Plan can include:*)

- Complete financial results including an accountant statement and copies of tax forms for past years

- Complete set of sales literature, brochures, catalogs, and so on

- Resumes from key managers

- Detailed monthly pro forma sales forecast, personnel plan, profit and loss, cash flow, and balance sheet

- Competitive advertisements

7

Licensing

Modern paper was invented in China around 105 AD by T'sai Lun. Quill pens have been used for 1,000 years, but the first successful fountain pen did not appear until 1884. The pen was later improved upon by Philo Remington's typewriter in 1873.

Today's word processor makes us wonder how we ever recorded history at all.

Your invention's evolution — from concept to market — involves substantial time, money, and effort. In the challenging process of taking an idea and turning it into something of value, licensing may be one way to reward your efforts and ease the burden.

Licensing to an established corporation provides numerous advantages over trying to sell your product yourself. Manufacturing companies offer an existing ability to make the product along with the means to distribute it, including their advertising experience and resources. They can provide name recognition of the company and penetration of domestic and foreign markets.

1. What Is a Licensing Agreement?

A licensing agreement is a contract between you (the inventor or licensor), who authorizes a buyer (licensee) to use your property, patent, trademark, copyright, or any form of intellectual property for compensation. It's a special kind of contract that benefits both the licensor and the licensee. (See Sample 2 at the end of this chapter for an example of a license agreement.)

Licensing grants only limited rights to the property to the licensee, usually for a fixed period of time, and often for a specified use or market for sale. For example, you might sign an agreement licensing your product for one year, or perhaps within a certain geographic area only. If you sign an exclusive license, then there are no limitations on where the licensee can sell your property.

You can license a product many times over (if it's not an exclusive license). Your ownership provides you with an asset whose value is determined by what a potential licensee will pay you for it. That also means that you can sue anyone who tries to infringe on your rights.

Licensing can provide you with income for a long time, with much less risk and commitment than is involved in raising investment capital, manufacturing, and dealing with all the aspects of establishing and owning a company that produces and sells a product. However, because you are handing over to the licensee the risk of investment and establishing the product in the market, you are also handing over some of the potential income. As a licensor, you will only receive a small percentage of the profit from the sales of a licensed product or technology. The licensee must make the required investment in establishing everything necessary to produce the finished product and get it to the buyer or end user.

Besides the benefits of royalties in licensing, in many cases you may be offered equity in a new business venture, especially if it is being created for the purpose of marketing the finished product that is the result of the license. The percentage often depends on the level of commitment and the benefits to the venture that the inventor brings to the table, along with the position and responsibility.

2. A Reality Check

Before you seek a licensee, you must have a realistic picture of what your product is worth. When I worked with inventors on a daily basis, I discovered that many thought their idea was worth a million dollars, even though most were untested and not patented.

When someone told me that his or her idea was worth a million dollars, I put that person through an exercise to get him or her to seriously consider the worth of the product. First, I would tell him or her that I knew someone who was interested in investing $500,000, and would be interested in looking at the idea. When presented with the prospect of meeting someone with this kind of money to invest, the inventor was almost always willing to reduce the product's worth.

After discussing their prospects further, I would then tell the inventor that setting up a meeting with the guy with the half million dollars would take months. I did, however, know a local investor with a quarter million dollars that he or she could meet with in a couple of weeks. It never failed that the first guy was dropped like a hot potato and the inventor's sights were now set on the second investor.

After a short time, I would tell the inventor that I could not guarantee success with either of these investors. I then presented another option of a local investor who needed to invest in something quickly so he could get out of paying taxes. Would the inventor be interested in talking to him, even though he didn't have as much money to invest? Without exception, the inventor wanted to meet this person.

At this point I would stop and explain what I had just done. The inventor would realize that he or she had been talked down from a million dollars to a much smaller undisclosed sum in a matter of minutes. This exercise helped many inventors realize that the true worth of their invention was negotiable.

3. Preliminary Considerations

Before looking for a prospective licensee or going to the table to negotiate a licensing agreement, you have to decide what it is you want out of the deal. Many inventors find licensing negotiations very intimidating and may lose certain bargaining points because of their inexperience. I highly recommend that you seek legal assistance to negotiate a licensing contract that is designed to fit your specific situation and needs. What you pay a lawyer for helping you with the negotiations may well be worth it for what you get in return.

In order to proceed to the licensing stage, you should have as a minimum a US patent application filed to cover your idea. A working model of the product is also very important. A product that is already selling on the market is worth more and can be licensed more easily. If you have done test marketing with small production runs, you can seek out a licensing agreement on this basis.

The value of a product is determined by what a company is willing to pay for it. The true value of a licensable technology, idea, or patent must be based on the perceived value to the licensee. If they recognize how it fits into their business, and what it can do for their sales and profits, they are likely to value the product more highly and be more generous in the licensing negotiations.

Before you enter into any negotiation, ask yourself what royalty percentage you want. (Five percent is generally a good starting point for the inventor who is receiving up-front money as well.) Also, are you going to ask for any up-front money? This can be negotiated and may be a trade-off for higher royalties.

4. Finding a Licensee

The first step in licensing is, of course, finding someone who is interested in your idea or product. Finding a licensee is much like many of the other steps in developing your idea. You must decide what you want, research your prospects, and then go after it. Your chance of licensing your idea will depend greatly upon how well you've completed each development and marketing stage.

The business of licensing must be approached seriously and recognized as an opportunity with great rewards if handled properly and professionally. As with any other part of your product development, you must always present a professional image. This means dressing professionally, being on time for meetings, and being prepared.

The research objective is to compile a list of potential licensees and to prioritize them based upon their potential value to you. Unless the product fits into a niche market, you must find a company that is financially stable and has the ability to take your product to market. Large corporations quite often do not seek or have any interest in acquiring technology from outside their own research laboratories. However, they do present the advantage of being more likely to offer a license agreement that is properly drafted, with minimum guaranteed royalties, and benchmark performance criteria defined.

If you are presently marketing your idea, even in a limited fashion, your idea has much greater merit, and you may have had inquiries already from your competitors about licensing arrangements. If you have a truly unique product, licensing can be as simple as checking out the store aisles where your competitors' products are found. Companies are always eager to expand their product lines into new areas, or to sell improved versions of currently available products. Nearly every package gives the name and location of its producer.

The next step is to research the company at the library. The best place to start looking for a licensee is within the industry with which your product is associated. The *Thomas Register* is an excellent source for names. Writing letters to prospective licensees can take time. If you have not done any marketing, it may be time to start publicizing that your product is up for license, as well as approaching your business contacts.

The local Chamber of Commerce and business support centers are a good source of leads. Contacting local venture capitalists or banks can provide additional possibilities. Remember, industry needs new products. It's a matter of being seen by those seeking something new and innovative.

You can also consult *Dun & Bradstreet's Reference Book of Corporate Management*, which gives a detailed biographical description of more than 75,000 principal officers of more than 12,000 leading companies. It supplies names, titles, and an array of vital statistics.

Standard & Poor's *Register of Corporations, Directors and Executives* lists 45,000 corporations along with their executives, and detailed information on some 450,000 potential licensee contacts.

Other good sources are the *Million Dollar Directory* and the *Middle Market Directory*, both from Dun & Bradstreet, listing thousands of companies, each with assets exceeding $500,000.

Any communication with a potential licensee should be directed to top management — the president or chief executive officer. Although letters are many times first screened by secretaries, professional-looking communications will almost always draw attention to you and your product.

Inventors are usually at their most vulnerable at this stage. Be careful in thinking that the first interested party will be your last. You will likely feel as though you've come too far to miss the boat now, and you may make a hasty decision in signing a contract. Try not to get too excited, feeling that you're lucky just to have someone talking to you. Keep in mind that it is the licensee who is also taking the risk and adjust your thinking accordingly.

You will, unfortunately, receive your share of "we're not interested" letters. But for now, just put them aside for future reference.

5. Meeting with a Potential Licensee

A successful first meeting with a potential licensee is crucial to your licensing effort — you are not only promoting your product, but also promoting yourself as knowledgeable and professional. Before the meeting, it's important to research the company to understand the background and current market needs. You also want to feel comfortable with the company and to find out if you can trust them.

Here are some points you should be prepared to cover in an initial meeting:

- Describe the demand for the product and how you have determined the demand. Include market research and testing.

- Discuss all the applications and alternatives to the product.

- Demonstrate why the licensee will benefit from your product, and discuss the innovation presently on the market.

- Discuss potential patents, trademarks, and copyrights.

- Explain your qualifications for inventing the product, emphasizing your business background.

6. Licensing Contacts

Sample 6 is an example of a licensing contract favoring the inventor. This sample is a guide only, but it can help you in comparing other contracts that may lean toward the licensee. Licensing agreements are subject to various tax laws, state and federal securities laws, and other laws, which impact on business. They may also be subject to state and federal franchise laws, antitrust laws, and case law. To be safe, check with your legal adviser.

6.1 Terms of the contract

There are numerous ways an agreement can be structured. For example, you may want to have one company manufacture the product and another company distribute it. As well, you can limit where the rights apply to geographically. The license agreement can include only the United States, or the whole world. My first product was licensed in the United States, Canada, and South America. Surprisingly, South America turned out to be my biggest market.

Probably the most important term of the license agreement to you, at least at this point, will be you how much your royalties will be and when they will be paid to you. Royalties commonly are expressed as a percentage of the licensee's net sales price of the licensed product. Typically, a royalty is from 1 to 10 percent depending on many different factors. A very important factor that will influence the royalty rate is the strength and scope of the patent protection, and the additional values such as a trademark.

The stage of the development is also a big factor. The licensee will want to know how much money must be invested in more research to determine the finished product. The royalty can also vary depending upon your granting an exclusive or non-exclusive license.

The agreement should specify if you are to receive any up-front money. It may also have a clause providing for a minimum performance to make sure that the company does what they say they are going to do.

6.2 The language of contracts and licenses

Before you begin negotiating a licensing agreement, take the time to become familiar with the terms and language you are likely to encounter. Understanding these terms now may help you protect your ideas and avoid lawsuits later. Here are the most common terms used along with some pointers on what to watch out for:

- **Derivative works:** Any refinement or modification to your product. If not properly defined, an improvement on your product could become their product, not yours, to license. Many contracts are weak in this area, and it is your responsibility to ensure that any product improvement made by others is included in your product and that the altered product remains your property.

- **Exclusivity:** The right to exclusive sales or distribution within a certain time or geographical area. National or even worldwide exclusivity rights can be a strong negotiating position and should not be bargained away easily. Use exclusivity as a bargaining chip and remember, if you found one licensee, you can find more.

- **Gross profits:** The net sales price less the cost of raw materials, labor, manufacturing, shipping, and packaging. Many different costs may be subtracted from the gross profits. Be very careful about labor cost, because a manufacturer or investor can take back all their investment in the product and claim a tax write-off. This costing must be defined and controlled now, or your royalties may pay the investor's brother $100,000 a year to box the product.

- **Licensed devices:** This explains exactly what the invention consists of and limits the scope of the agreement to only that product. Look to the future; you may be in another business later and may want to license to another industry.

- **Licensed patents:** This includes the patent number and claims, or gives an explanation beyond that detailed under licensed devices. If a patent is pending, detail what happens if you are not granted a patent, because it could happen.

- **Minimum royalty:** Details the minimum amount of royalty you will receive at certain intervals. It should say you will get paid, no matter what problems the licensee may encounter.

- **Payment:** Details how much is paid to you and to others, and when. It should include a late penalty and a time limit for payments or royalties, and should detail what happens when payments are not met. You should include a cut-off point for late payments where all rights revert back to you, and a statement that any partial payments are nonrefundable.

- **Performance:** A performance clause simply stating the minimum number of units that should be sold within a specified period of time. A performance clause works well as an anti-shelving clause, and it should explain in detail what happens if sales expectation is not met. The anti-shelving clause is a means of keeping interest in your product, as the licensee will be paying royalties to you even if the product never reaches the market. After a certain time, all rights should revert back to you. If this is not clearly set out in writing, you will have to go to court to win back your invention.

- **Records and reports:** Define the type of records to be kept, and also allow for an independent audit, which helps keep everyone honest. It should also indicate whether the investor is entitled to review records, which can be important in estimating royalties.

- **Research and development:** This defines the effort to stay ahead of the competition and should even include fees to be paid to the inventor for further research.

- **Third-party infringement:** A clause detailing what happens if someone tries to infringe on your idea should be included. Infringement can cause much hardship, and the license agreement must specify who will fight the lawsuits. The licensee will consider it the inventor's problem, yet the business could fail if the inventor is poorly financed. Be careful of the wording.

- **Sublicensing:** A quick way for the inventor to lose all control if not restricted by the original contract. If the contract does not restrict sublicensing, you could find yourself competing with your own product shipped from another country.

- **Term:** The length of time the license will run.

- **Termination and abandonment:** Specifies what happens if everything falls through. Make sure that in a licensing agreement you have no responsibility to pay back company loans. State clearly that you receive all rights to improvements should the contract fail.

- **Up-front payment:** Money paid at the time of signing. Negotiating for up-front money will depend largely upon the product and how badly the licensee wants it. I have signed deals where as much as $50,000 was paid up-front, so it can be done. The licensee may argue that he has to invest in molds, engineering, testing, and start-up. Your argument, of course, is that the money is required to reimburse out-of-pocket expenses for development, prototyping, patenting, and other costs. Additionally, up-front money will sometimes make the licensee work a little harder to recoup his or her investment.

A sound licensing agreement will benefit both you and the licensee, but it's only as good as the integrity of those who sign it. Don't forget to read the fine print — if it looks too good to be true, it usually is.

7. Negotiating an Agreement

While negotiating a licensing agreement for your invention, it pays to stay cool and view things from all possible angles. Taking time to think clearly now will help you avoid licensing what could result in a future lawsuit. Litigation can take years to settle and cost you dearly before you recover any money, if ever.

Licensing may or may not be for you. A successful license may also change very rapidly after problems arise in the marketplace. Consider if you want up-front money verses royalties. Many products look great, but do not sell as well as expected. Poor product performance can come as a surprise, but happens all too often.

This is not meant to discourage you, but to emphasize the reality of the marketplace. The world is hungry for new products, and devours them at the rate of more than 10,000 a year. Many do not have any protection and are copied quickly. Many are licensed and still get copied.

Due to the complexity of the subject, only a few legal considerations of licensing have been discussed. It is always advisable to look into local and state restrictions when signing any legal document. Many inventors will fall into unfamiliar territory when negotiating a license and could fail to follow local or state antitrust and securities laws. Seriously consider legal counsel when getting ready to sign on the dotted line.

Resources

These are some organizations that deal with licensing issues:

- The National Venture Capital Association (NVCA)

- The National Association of Small Business Investment Companies (NASBIC)

- International Licensing Industry Association

SAMPLE 2
License Agreement

License Agreement

This agreement is made between

_____ ("Licensor") and

_____("Licensee")

on _____, 20 ____. Licensor is the sole inventor and owner of

_____ ("Intellectual Property")

including but not limited to certain information, technical data, processes, know-how, stop practices, drawings, plans, specifications, methods of manufacture, trademarks, and other data herein after known as the invention. Licensee desires to obtain a nonexclusive license to utilize the information and to manufacture and sell the invention. In consideration of the mutual promises in this agreement, the parties agree as follows and defined herein:

1. Scope. This agreement shall be limited to the product and information known as the invention.

2. License. Subject to the terms of this agreement, Licensor grants to Licensee the nonexclusive, nontransferable right and license to use the information to manufacture the invention and sell or lease the invention within the United States. No license, expressed or implied, is granted to employ the information for any other purpose whatsoever.

3. Compensation.

SAMPLE 2 — Continued

A. Payment. The consideration due and payable to Licensor for the rights granted to Licensee hereunder shall be the sum of $_____ us dollars due and payable on execution of this agreement.

B. Further Consideration. As further consideration for the grants of this license provides for hereunder, Licensee agrees to spend no less than $_____ for the purpose of manufacturing, distribution, and promotion of the invention before six months from the date of execution of this agreement.

C. Royalties. In addition to the consideration due and payable to Licensor, Licensee agrees to assume and pay royalties on all licensed devices sold equal to _____ percent of the gross profits realized from the exploration and rights to the licensed invention.

D. Payment Schedule. After _____ 20____. Payments of royalties shall be paid to Licensor with each quarterly report.

4. Records. Licensee shall maintain accurate records relating to the manufacturing and sale of the invention. Licensee shall render quarterly reports to Licensor within three weeks of the end of each quarter showing the total quantity of inventions produced; the quantity sold, leased or otherwise utilized; the gross receipts received by Licensor for such transactions; and the amounts due Licensor as royalties. Licensor or an authorized representative shall have the right to inspect and copy such records and books of account upon Licensor's written request, and such inspection and copying shall be done during Licensee's regular business hours.

5. Research and Development. Licensee shall make funds available for the further research, development, and improvements and derivative works of the invention. Funds shall be no less than $_____ per year. All improvements and derivative works of the invention shall be included within this agreement.

6. Termination of the agreement.

SAMPLE 2 — Continued

A. Unless terminated sooner, this agreement shall remain in force through _____, 20_____.

B. Either party shall have the right to terminate this agreement if the other fails to perform per written agreement herein, provided that such failure shall not have been remedied by the defaulting party within 60 days of having received written notice of intention to terminate.

C. Bankruptcy or Insolvency of Licensee shall automatically terminate this agreement with all rights returning to Licensor.

D. Licensee shall have the right to sell or lease any products on hand or contracted for as of the date of termination. Any termination shall not release Licensee from payment of royalties accrued through the date of termination.

7. This agreement shall be interpreted in accordance with the laws of the State of _____.

8. Licensee agrees to make adequate warning for the product, and comply with all applicable laws and regulations.

9. Licensee agrees to carry third-party liability insurance to insure and adequately cover both Licensor and Licensee against claims resulting from damage or personal injury through sale or use of the product (Invention). Licensee agrees to make Licensor as an additional insured on such insurance policies.

10. No terms of this agreement can be modified or waived except in writing signed by both parties.

11. Service of notice as provided for in this agreement shall be given in writing and shall be considered duly served and given by mailing the same, postage prepaid by registered mail to the parties at the following addresses:

_____

_____

_____

SAMPLE 2 — Continued

and

_____

_____

_____

12. A minimum royalty shall be paid to Licensor of $_____ per month for the first six months after execution of agreement and $_____ per month from the seventh month on.

13. Licensee shall permit, during normal business hours, a duly authorized representative of the Licensor, or Licensor to enter Licensee premises for the purpose of ascertaining that the Licensee is complying with the provisions of this agreement.

14. Nothing herein shall be construed as a warranty or representation given by Licensor to Licensee attesting to the scope or validity of the herein named patent application or any patent issuing thereon.

15. Third-Party Infringement suits shall be entered into equally with Licensor monies transferred from future royalties if necessary. Said settlement shall be equally divided between Licensee and Licensor.

In witness whereof the parties hereto have hereunto signed their respective names and affixed their respective corporate seal.

_____ ("Licensor")

_____ ("Licensee")

Executed this _____ day of _____, 20 _____

8

Conclusion

The purpose of your reading this book grew from the exercise of your own creativity. Being creative is an integral part of you; it's a gift. Even though we may not be consciously aware of it at the time, almost everything we learn about the world teaches us a little more about ourselves. In the same way, learning about our creativity can help us to understand ourselves and the world.

Creative people find it exciting to develop new ideas and generate new products. What's intriguing is that people in our society generally don't like change, tending instead to cling to the status quo. Society as a whole discourages unconventional thought, attempting instead to force surrender of our unique, fundamentally creative selves to an accepted conformity.

Curiously, certain people are able to resist this pressure and rise above the limitations society imposes. They welcome into their experience the inconsistencies and contradictions of a complex world, and their observations are enriched in the process. As inventors, the world offers us problems to solve. The more we know about a problem, the easier it is to find a solution. The creative observer sees the possibilities of new combinations of both existing and newly conceived ideas.

Communicating your idea is the beginning of the design process..

Being creative is an important aspect of developing your idea, but it's easy to lose sight of this ability when dealing with the world of manufacturing and marketing, where the bottom line dictates success or failure. To be successful, your creative ability must now be channeled, not to the abstract, but to the specific, concrete steps required to develop your product and take it to market.

These challenges will require a new application of your creativity — towards solving the many problems encountered in developing a product, including testing of your design, materials selection, manufacturing processes, assembly methods, distribution, sales, licensing, financing, and most importantly, providing distinct value to the customer who validates your original idea by buying the product.

Ideas have no value or meaning outside the mind in which they are conceived until they are communicated to others. Creativity is also needed in the communication required to obtain the support necessary to bring your idea to reality. Communicating your idea is the beginning of the design process, the most important part of the development of a new product.

The knowledge in this book on intellectual property protection will give you the information you need to protect yourself. The methods of evaluation described will enhance your new product. The marketing research procedures outlined will guide you toward success.

But, most important, your success will depend on whether you can carry creativity as an integrated thread throughout all the stages of developing your idea. Can you do much more than just come up with an idea? Can you complete the many difficult steps required to take your product to market? Can you enter unfamiliar territory with an open mind, confident attitude, and hopeful spirit? Can you persevere when faced with rejection and disappointment? Can you defy the odds? Your creativity will be a beacon through this challenging and sometimes turbulent process.

I began my career as an inventor with nothing more than an idea. I always believed I could beat the odds. If you truly believe you can too, then the battle is half won already. Never give up! Good luck and keep on being creative.

Appendix

1. Inventors' Organizations

1.1 National organizations

United Inventors Association (UIA)
  PO Box 23447
  Rochester, NY 14692
  Tel: (585) 359-9310
  Fax: (585) 359-1132
  E-mail: IACUIA@aol.com
  www.uiausa.org/

National Congress of Inventor Organizations (NSIO)
  PO Box 931881
  Los Angeles, CA 90093-1881
  Tel: (323) 878-6952
  Fax: (213) 947-1079
  E-mail: ncio@inventionconvention.com
  www.inventionconvention.com/ncio

1.2 State organizations

ALABAMA

Invent Alabama
137 Mission Circle
Montevallo, AL 35115
Tel: (205) 663-9982
Fax: (205) 250-8013

Alabama Inventors Clubs
Francisco Guerra
c/o Snowmasters
3481 County Road 93
Anderson, AL 35610
Tel: (256) 229-5551

ALASKA

Alaska Inventors & Entrepreneurs
PO Box 241801
Anchorage, AK 99524-1801
Tel/fax: (907) 563-4337
E-mail: inventor@arctic.net
www.arctic.net/~inventor/

Inventors Institute of Alaska
Al Jorgensen
PO Box 876154
Wasilla, AK 99687
Tel: (907) 376-5114

ARIZONA

Inventor's Association of Arizona (IAA)
PO Box 6436
Glendale, AZ 85312
Tel: (520) 751-9966
E-mail: wonderworker@qwest.net
www.azinventors.org

ARKANSAS

Inventors Congress Inc.
Garland Bull
Rt2 — Box 1630
Dandanell, AR 72834
Tel: (501) 229-4515

CALIFORNIA

Inventors Forum
PO Box 8008
Huntington Beach, CA 92615-8008
Tel: (714) 540-2491
www.inventorsforum.org

Inventors Alliance
PO BOX 390219
Mountain View, CA 94039-390219
Tel: (650) 964-1576
Fax: (650) 964-1576
www.inventorsalliance.org/

Central Valley Inventor's Association
PO Box 1551
Manteca, CA 95336
Tel/Fax: (209) 239-5414
E-mail: cdesigns@softcom.net

Inventors Forum of San Diego
11292 Poblado Road
San Diego, CA 92127
Tel: (858) 451-1028
Fax: (858) 451-6154

InventNET
PO Box 11381
Westminster, CA 92685-1381
www.inventnet.com

Idea to Market Network
PO Box 12248
Santa Rosa, CA 95406
Tel: 1-800-ITM-3210
E-mail: info@ideatomarket.org
www.ideatomarket.org

Bruce Sawyer Center
520 Mendocino Ave., Suite 210
Santa Rosa, CA 95401
Tel: (707) 524-1773

American Inventor Network
1320 High School Road
Sebastopol, CA 95472
Tel: (707) 823-3865
Fax: (707) 823-0913

The Inventors Alliance of Northern California (IANC)
22070 Palo Way STE 4
Redding, CA 96049-3365
Tel: (530) 243-2400
E-mail: ianc@frontiernet.net
www.inventorsnorcal.org

COLORADO

Rocky Mountain Inventors Association (RMIA)
Po Box 280475
Lakewood, CO 80228-0475
Tel: (303) 670-3760 (Answering Service)
Fax: (720) 962-5026
E-mail: info@RMinventor.org
www.rminventor.org

CONNECTICUT

Innovators Guild
2 Worden Road
Danbury, CT 06811
Tel: (203) 790-8235

Christian Inventors Association
7 Woonsocket Avenue
Shelton, CT 06484
Tel: (203) 924-9538
E-mail: pal@ourpal.com

Inventors Association of Connecticut
46 Rutland Avenue
Fairfield, CT 06825
Tel: (203) 331-9696
E-mail: bob@distinti.com
www.inventus.org

Manufacturing Applications Center
Central Connecticut State University
185 Main Street
New Britain, CT 06051
Tel: (860) 827-7875
www.macteam.org

DELAWARE

Early Stage East
3 Mill Road, Ste 201A
Wilmington, DE 19806
Tel: (302) 777-2460
E-mail: info@earlystageeast.org
www.earlystageeast.org

DISTRICT OF COLUMBIA

Inventors Network of the Capital Area (INCA)
PO Box 15150
Arlington, VA 22215
Tel: (703) 971-9216
www.dcinventors.org

FLORIDA

Edison Inventors Association, Inc.
PO Box 07398
Ft. Myers, FL 33919
Tel: (941) 275-4332
www.edisoninventors.org

Tampa Bay Inventors Council
10750 Endeavour Way
Largo, FL 33777
Tel/Fax: (727) 481-7605
www.tbic.us

Space Coast Inventors Guild
Angel Pacheco
1221 Pine Tree Drive
Indian Harbour Beach, FL 32937
Tel/Fax: (321) 773-4031

Inventors Council of Central Florida
4855 Big Oaks Lane
Orlando, FL 32806-7826
Tel: (407) 859-4855
Fax: (407) 438-3922

Inventors Society of South Florida
PO Box 4306
Boynton, FL 33424
Tel: (954) 486-2426

Palm Isles Inventors Group
9528 Shadybrook Drive, Ste. 102
Boynton Beach, FL 33437-6138
Tel: (561) 739-9259 or 9439

GEORGIA

Inventor Associates of Georgia, Inc.
Secretary, Inventor Associates of Georgia
1608 Pelham Way
Macon, GA 31220
Tel: (912) 474-6948
www.geocities.com/iaggroup

HAWAII

Hawaii-International Inventors Association, Inc.
945 Makaiwa Street
Honolulu, HI 96816
Tel: (808) 523-5555
Fax: (808) 538-3168

IDAHO

East Idaho Inventors Forum
Po Box 452
Shelley, ID 83274
Tel: (208) 346-6763

ILLINOIS

Illinois Innovators & Inventor's Club
PO Box 623
Edwardsville, IL 62025
Tel: (618) 656-7445
E-mail: Invent@Charter-IL.com

INDIANA

Indiana Inventors Association
5514 South Adams
Marion, IN 46953
Tel: (765) 674-2845
Fax: (765) 733-0579

IOWA

Drake University Inventure Program
2507 University Avenue
Des Moines, IA 50311
Tel: (515) 271-2655

KANSAS

Inventors Association of South Central Kansas (IASCK)
2302 North Amarado Street
Wichita, KS 67205
Tel: (316) 721-1866
www.inventkansas.com

Kansas Association of Inventors
272 W 6th Street
Hoisington, KS 67544
Tel: (316) 653-2165

Mid-America Inventors Association, Inc.
PO Box 2778
Kansas City, KS 66110
Tel: (913) 371-7011
E-mail: midamerica-inventors@kc.rr.com
www.midamerica-inventors.com

KENTUCKY

Central Kentucky Inventors Council, Inc.
Mark Miller
3055 Williams Lane
Versailles, KY 40383
Tel: (859) 879-1895

LOUISIANA

No Listings

MAINE

Portland Inventors Forum
Department Industrial Cooperation
University of Maine
5717 Corbet Hall, Room 430
Orono, ME 04469-5717
Tel: (207) 581-2200
Fax: (207) 581-1479
www.umaine.edu/DIC

MARYLAND

Inventors Network of the Capital Area (INCA)
PO Box 15150
Arlington, VA 22215
Tel: (703) 971-9216
www.dcinventors.org

MASSACHUSETTS

Inventors' Association of New England (IANE)
PO Box 355
Lexington, MA 02420-0004
Tel: (978) 369-7074
www.inventne.org/

Innovators' Resource Network
PO Box 137
Shutesbury, MA 01072-0137
Tel: (413) 259-2006
E-mail: info@IRNetwork.org
www. irnetwork.org
(Group Meets in Springfield, MA)

Cape Cod Inventors Association
Briar Main — PO Box 143
Wellfleet, MA 02667
Tel: (508) 349-1629

MICHIGAN

Inventors' Council of Mid-Michigan
58169 Dulwich
Washingtontownship, MI 48094
Tel: (586) 980-9630
www.inventorscouncil.com

InventorEd, Inc.
1323 West Cook Road
Grand Blanc, MI 48439
E-mail: HELP@InvEd.org
www.inventored.org/

Inventors Clubs of America
524 Curtis Road
E. Lansing, MI 48823
Tel: (517) 332-3561

Inventors Association of Metropolitan Detroit
24405 Gratiot Ave.
Eastpointe, MI 48021-3306
Tel: (810) 772-7888

The Entrepreneur Network
350 Corrie Road
Ann Arbor, MI 48105
Tel: 1-800-468-8871
E-mail: edzimmer@TENonline.org
http://tenonline.org

MINNESOTA

Society of Minnesota Inventors
20231 Basalt St. NW
Anoka, MN 55303
Tel: (763) 753-2766

Inventors' Network
23 Empire Drive
St. Paul, MN 55103
Tel: (651) 602-3175
www.inventorsnetwork.org

Minnesota Inventors Congress
PO Box 71
Redwood Falls, MN 56283
Tel: (507) 537-64768
Toll free: 1-800-468-3681
Fax: (507) 537-6094
E-mail: mic@southwestmsu.edu
www.invent1.org

MISSISSIPPI

Mississippi Inventor Assistance
B19 Jeanette Phillips Drive
University, MS 38677
Tel: (662) 915-5001 or 1-800-725-7232 (for use in MS only)
E-mail: msbdc@olemiss.edu
www.olemiss.edu/depts/mssbdc/invent.html

MISSOURI

Center for Business & Economic Development
University of SW Missouri State
901 S National Avenue
Springfield, MO 65804
Tel: (417) 836-5671

Inventors Association of St. Louis (IASL)
1640 South Lindbergh Blvd.
St. Louis, MO 63131
Tel: (314) 432-1291

Women's Inventor Project
7400 Foxmount
Hazlewood, MO 63042
Tel: (905) 731-0328

MONTANA

Montana Inventors Association
5350 Love Lane
Bozeman, MT 59715
Tel: (406) 586-1541
Fax: (406) 585-9028

NEBRASKA

Lincoln Inventors Association
92 Ideal Way
Brainard, NE 68626
Tel/fax: (402) 545-2179

NEVADA

Nevada Inventors Association
PO Box 11008
Reno, NV 89506
Tel: (775) 677-4824
Fax: (775) 677-4888
www.nevadainventors.org

Inventors Society of Southern Nevada
3627 Huerta Drive
Las Vegas, NV 89121
Tel/fax: (702) 435-7741
E-Mail: InventSSN@aol.com

NEW HAMPSHIRE
No Listings

NEW JERSEY

Kean University SBDC
215 North Avenue, Room 242
Union, NJ 07083
Tel: (908) 737-5950
Fax: (908) 737-5955

National Society of Inventors
94 North Rockledge Drive
Livingston, NJ 07039-1121
Tel: (973) 994-9282
Fax: (973) 535-0777
www.nationalinventors.com

New Jersey Entrepreneurs Forum, Inc.
PO Box 313
Westfield, NJ 07090
Tel: (908) 789-3424
www.njef.org

NEW MEXICO

New Mexico Inventors Club
PO Box 30062
Albuquerque, NM 87190
Tel/fax: (505) 266-3541

NEW YORK

Binghamton Innovators Network
65 Hospital Hill Road
Binghamton, NY 13901
Tel: (607) 648-4626

NY Society of Professional Inventors
Box 216
Farmingdale, NY 11735-9996
Tel: (516) 799-1362
www.geocites.com/nyspi2001/

Long Island Forum for Technology,
111 West Main Street
Bay Shore, NY 11706
Tel: (631) 969-3700
Fax: (631) 969-4489
E-mail: info@lift.org
www.lift.org

Inventors Society of Western New York
52 Manor Hill Drive
Fairport, NY 14450
Tel: (585) 223-1225
E-mail: inventnewyork@aol.com

The Aurora Club
Richard Guard
11880 Centerline Road
South Wales, NY 14139 (located Southeast of Buffalo)
Tel: (716) 652-4704
E-mail: guardunlimited@aol.com

NORTH DAKOTA

Northern Plains Inventors Congress
2534 South University Drive, Suite 4
Fargo, ND 58103
Toll free: 1-800-281-7009
Fax: (701) 237-0544
www.ndinventors.com

OHIO

Inventors Connection Greater Cleveland, Inc.
PO Box 360804
Cleveland, OH 44136
Tel: (216) 226-9681
E-mail: icgc@usa.com
http://members.aol.com/icgc/

Inventors Council of Canton
303 55th Street NW
North Canton, OH 44720
Tel: (330) 499-1262
E-Mail: President@InventorsCouncilofCanton.org
inventorscouncilofcanton.org

Youngstown-Warren Inventors Association
351 Florine Ave.
Leavittsburg, OH 44430
Tel: (330) 898-2560
http://home.neo.rr.com/fmnaypaver/invwell.htm

Inventors' Council of Cincinnati
PO Box 70
Milford, OH 45150
Tel: (513) 831-0664
http://inventorscouncil.tripod.com/home/index.htm

Inventors Network, Inc.
1275 Kinnear Road
Columbus, OH 43212
Tel: (614) 470-0144
E-mail: 13832667@msn.com

Inventors Council of Dayton
PO Box 611
Dayton, OH 45409
Tel: (937) 256-9698
www.daytoninventors.com

OKLAHOMA

Oklahoma Inventors Congress
PO Box 57464
Oklahoma City, OK 73112
Tel: (405) 947-5782
Fax: (405) 947-6950
www.oklahomainvestors.com

OREGON

South Oregon Inventors Council
332 W. 6th Street
Medford, OR 97501
Tel: (541) 772-3478
Fax: (541) 734-4813

South Coast Inventors Group
2455 Maple Leaf
North Bend, OR 97459
Tel: (541) 756-6866
Fax: (541) 756-5735

Inventors Group at Umpqua Community College SBDC
744 SE Rose Street
Roseburg, OR 97470
Contact: Walt Bammann
Tel: (541) 673-8309 (call after 3 p.m.)
E-mail: wbamman@wizzards.net

PENNSYLVANIA

American Society of Inventors
PO Box 58426
Philadelphia, PA 19102
Tel: (215) 546-6601
www.asoi.org

Pennsylvania Inventors Association
2317 East 43rd Street
Erie, PA 16510
Tel: (814) 825-5820
www.painventors.org

Central Pennsylvania Inventors Association
117 N. 20th Street
Camp Hill, PA 17011
Tel: (717) 763-5742

RHODE ISLAND

The Center for Design & Business
169 Weybosset St., 2nd Floor
Providence, RI 02903
Tel: (401) 454-6108
Fax: (401) 454-6559
www.centerdesignbusiness.org

SOUTH CAROLINA

Carolina Inventors Council
108 Monarch Place
Taylors, SC 29687
Tel: (864) 268-9892

TENNESSEE

Inventors' Association of Middle Tennessee
3908 Trimble Rd.
Nashville, TN 37215
Tel: (615) 269-4346

Tennessee Inventors Assn.
PO Box 11225
Knoxville, TN 37939-1225
Tel: (865) 981-2927
www.uscni.com/tia

TEXAS

Houston Inventors Association
2916 West TC Jester Blvd., Suite 100
Houston, TX 77018
Tel/Fax: (713) 686-7676
www.inventors.org

Technology Advocates of San Antonio
112 East Pecan, Suite 100
San Antonio, TX 78205
Tel: (210) 246-5995
Fax: (210) 246-5999
www.tasa.org

Texas Inventors Association
PO Box 251248
Plano, TX 75025
www.asktheinventors.com

Amarillo Inventors Association
7000 West 45th
Amarillo, TX 79109
Tel: (806) 352-6085
Fax: (806) 352-6264

UTAH

University of Utah
Engineering Experiment Station
1495 East 100 South, Room 138
Salt Lake City, UT 84112
Tel: (801) 581-6348
www.utah.edu/uees/

VERMONT

Inventors Network of Vermont
4 Park Street
Springfield, VT 05156
Tel: (802) 885-5100 or (802) 885-8178

Invent Vermont
PO Box 82
Woodbury, VT 05681
Tel: (802) 879-7411
www.inventvermont.com

VIRGINIA

Inventors Network of the Capital Area
PO Box 15150
Arlington, VA 22215
Tel: (703) 971-9216
www.dcinventors.org

Blue Ridge Inventor's Club
PO Box 6701
Charlottesville, VA 22906-6701
Tel: (434) 973-3708
Fax: (434) 973-2004

WASHINGTON

Inventors Network
PO Box 5575
Vancouver, WA 98668
Tel: (503) 239-8299

WEST VIRGINIA
No Listings

WISCONSIN

Inventors Network of Wisconsin
1066 Saint Paul Street
Green Bay, WI 54304
Tel: (920) 429-0331

Central Wisconsin Inventors Association
PO Box 915
Manawa, WI 54949
Tel: (920) 596-3092

UW-Stout Incubator Service
UW-Stout Manufacturing Laboratory
Menomonie, WI 54751
Tel: (715) 232-2294

1.2 Canadian organizations

Inventors Alliance of Canada
350 Sunnyside Avenue
Toronto, ON M6R 2R6
Tel: (416) 410-7792
E-mail: info@investoralliance.com
www.inventorsalliance.com

Inventors Club of Brantford
73 Palace Street
Brantford, ON N3T 3W8
Tel: (519) 753-7735

British Columbia Inventors Society
PO Box 78055
Vancouver, BC V5N 5W1
Tel: (604) 707-0250
E-mail: info@bcinventor.com
www.bcinventor.com

Saskatchewan Research Council
125–15 Innovation Boulevard
Saskatoon, SK S7N 2X8
Tel: (306) 933-5400
www.src.sk.ca

Women Inventors Project
107 Holm Crescent
Thornhill, ON L3T5J4
Tel: (905) 731-0328
Fax: (905) 731-9691
www.womenip.com

2. Patent, Trademark, and Copyright Websites

National Patent Association
www.nationalpatent.com

National Inventor Fraud Center
www.inventorfraud.com

Self-help legal books
www.self-counsel.com

Inventors' Digest
www.inventorsdigest.com

International Trademark Association
www.inta.org

Inventor Resources
www.inventionconnection.com

Free e-mail for inventors
www.patentmail.com

United Inventors Association
www.uiausa.org

3. Patent Depository Libraries

ALABAMA

Auburn University Library
Auburn University
Auburn, AL 36849
Tel: (334) 844-1737

Birmingham Public Library
2100 Park Place
Birmingham, AL 35203
Tel: (205) 226-3610

ALASKA

Anchorage Municipal Libraries
Tel: (907) 562-7323

ARKANSAS

Arkansas State Library
One Capitol Mall
Little Rock, AR 72201
Tel: (501) 682-2053

CALIFORNIA

Los Angeles Public Library
630 West 5th Street
Los Angeles, CA 90071
Tel: (213) 228-7220

California State Library
Library Courts Building
900 N St.
Sacramento, CA 95814
Tel: (916) 654-0069

San Diego Public Library
820 East St.
San Diego, CA 92101
Tel: (619) 236-5813

San Francisco Public Library
100 Larkin St.
San Francisco, CA 94102
Tel: (415) 557-4500

COLORADO

Denver Public Library
10 West 14th Ave. Pkwy.
Denver, CO 80204
Tel: (720) 865-1711

CONNECTICUT

Connecticut State Library
Tel: (860) 695-6295

DELAWARE

University of Delaware Library
181 South College Ave.
Newark, DE 19717
Tel: (302) 831-2965

FLORIDA

Broward County Main Library
100 South Andrews Avenue
Fort Lauderdale, FL 33301
Tel: (954) 357-7444

Miami-Dade Public Library
101 West Flagler Street
Miami, FL 33130
Tel: (305) 357-2665

GEORGIA

Georgia Institute of Technology
704 Cherry St.
Atlanta, GA 30332
Tel: (404) 894-4529

HAWAII

Hawaii State Public Library
478 South King St.
Honolulu, HI 96813
Tel: (808) 586-3617

IDAHO

University of Idaho Library
Moscow, ID 83844
Tel: (208) 885-6235

ILLINOIS

Chicago Public Library
400 South State St.
Chicago, IL 60605
Tel: (312) 747-4450

Illinois State Library
300 South 2nd St.
Springfield, IL 62701
Tel: (217) 785-5600

INDIANA

Indianapolis-Marion County Public Library
40 East St. Clair Street
Indianapolis, IN 46206
Tel: (317) 269-1741

IOWA

State Library of Iowa
1112 East Grand Ave.
Des Moines, IA 50319
Tel: (515) 242-6541

KANSAS

Wichita State University
1845 Fairmount
Wichita, KS 67260-0068
Tel: (316) 978-3481

KENTUCKY

Louisville Free Public Library
301 York Street
Louisville, KY 40203
Tel: (502) 574-1611

LOUISIANA

Troy H. Middleton Library
Louisiana State University
Baton Rouge, LA 70803
Tel: (225) 578-8875

MAINE

University of Maine
Raymond H. Fogler Library
Orono, ME 04469
Tel: (207) 581-1678

MARYLAND

University of Maryland Library
University of Maryland
College Park, MD 20742
Tel: (301) 405-9157

MASSACHUSETTS

Boston Public Library
700 Boylston St.
Boston, MA 02116
Tel: (617) 536-5400

University of Massachusetts
Lederle Graduate Research Centre
740 North Pleasant St., 2nd Floor
Amherst, MA 01003
Tel: (413) 545-1370

MICHIGAN

University of Michigan
2281 Bonisteel Blvd.
Ann Arbor, MI 48109
Tel: (734) 647-5735

Detroit Public Library
5201 Woodward Avenue
Detroit, MI 48202
Tel: (313) 833-3379

MINNESOTA

Minneapolis Public Library
250 Marquette Ave.
Minneapolis, MN 55401
Tel: (612) 630-6000

MISSISSIPPI

Mississippi Library Commission
1221 Ellis Ave.
Jakson, MS 39209
Tel: (601) 961-4111

MISSOURI

Linda Hall Library
5109 Cherry Street
Kansas City, MO 64110
Tel: (816) 363-4600

St. Louis Public Library
1301 Olive Street
St. Louis, MO 63103
Tel: (314) 241-2288

MONTANA

Montana Tech Library
1300 West Park St.
Butte, MT 59701
Tel: (406) 496-4281

NEBRASKA

University of Nebraska
Lincoln Library
Lincoln, NE 68588
Tel: (402) 472-3411

NEVADA

University of Nevada-Reno
Reno, NV 89557
Tel: (775) 784-6579

NEW JERSEY

Newark Public Library
Main Library, 3rd Floor
5 Washington Street
Newark, NJ 07101
Tel: (973) 733-7779

NEW MEXICO

University of New Mexico General Library
Albuquerque, NM 87131
Tel: (505) 277-4412

NEW YORK

New York State Library
Cultural Education Center
Albany, NY 12230
Tel: (518) 474-5355

Buffalo and Erie County Public Library
1 Lafayette Square
Buffalo, NY 14203
Tel: (716) 858-8900

NORTH CAROLINA

North Carolina State University
The D.H. Hill Library
Raleigh, NC 27650
Tel: (919) 515-2935

NORTH DAKOTA

Chester Fritz Library
University of North Dakota
Rm 130A, 1st Floor W.
University Ave. and Centennial Dr.
Grand Forks, ND 58202
Tel: (701) 777-4888

OHIO

Public Library of Cincinnati and Hamilton County
800 Vine Street
Cincinnati, OH 45202
Tel: (513) 369-6971

Cleveland Public Library
325 Superior Avenue, NE
Cleveland, OH 44114
Tel: (216) 623-2870

Ohio State University Library
175 West 18th Ave.
Columbus, OH 43210
Tel: (614) 292-3022

Toledo Public Library
325 Michigan Street
Toledo, OH 43624
Tel: (419) 259-5209

OKLAHOMA

Oklahoma State University Library
5th Floor, Edmon Low Library
Stillwater, OK 74078
Tel: (405) 744-7086

OREGON

Portland State University Library
Lewis & Clark Law School
100 15 SW Terwilliger
Portland, OR 97219
Tel: (503) 768-6786

PENNSYLVANIA

Free Library of Pennsylvania
1901 Vine Street
Philadelphia, PA 19103
Tel: (215) 686-5331

Carnegie Library of Pittsburgh
4400 Forbes Avenue
Pittsburgh, PA 15213
Tel: (412) 622-3138

Pennsylvania State University
Paterno Library, 3rd Floor
University Park, PA 16802
Tel: (814) 865-6369

RHODE ISLAND

Providence Public Library
225 Washington St.
Providence, RI 02903
Tel: (401) 455-8027

SOUTH CAROLINA

Clemson University
R.M. Cooper Library
Clemson, SC 29634
Tel: (864) 656-3024

SOUTH DAKOTA

Devereaux Library
South Dakota School of Mines & Technology
501 East St. Joseph St.
Rapid City, SD 57701-3995
Tel: (605) 394-1275

TENNESSEE

Vanderbilt University Library
419 21st Ave. S.
Nashville, TN 37240
Tel: (615) 343-7105

TEXAS

University of Texas at Austin
Enginering Library
Austin, TX 78713
Tel: (512) 495-4500

Texas A & M University
College Station, TX 77843-5000
Tel: (979) 845-5745

Dallas Public Library
1515 Young Street
Dallas, TX 75201
Tel: (214) 670-1468

Rice University
The Fondren Library
Houston, TX 77251-1892
Tel: (713) 348-5483

UTAH

University of Utah
295 South 1500 E.
Salt Lake City, UT 84112
Tel: (801) 581-8394

VERMONT

Bailey/Howe Library
University of Vermont,
Burlington, VT
Tel: (802) 656-2542

VIRGINIA

Virginia Commonwealth University Library
901 Park Avenue
Richmond, VA 23284
Tel: (804) 828-1104

WASHINGTON

University of Washington
Engineering Library
Seattle, WA 98195
Tel: (206) 543-0740

WEST VIRGINIA

Evansdale Library
West Virginia University
Morgantown, WV 26506
Tel: (304) 293-4696

WISCONSIN

University of Wisconsin
Kurt F. Wendt Engineering Library
215 N. Randall Avenue
Madison, WI 53706
Tel: (608) 262-6845

Milwaukee Public Library
814 W. Wisconsin Avenue
Milwaukee, WI 53233
Tel: (414) 286-3051

WYOMING

Wyoming State Library
2301 Capitol Avenue
Cheyenne, WY 82002
Tel: (307) 777-7281

4. Industrial Application Centers

Indianapolis Center for Advanced Research
611 N. Capitol Avenue
Indianapolis, IN 46204
Tel: (317) 264-3745
www.indiana.edu/~ovpr/ctrdir/icar.html

Central Industrial Applications Center/NASA (CIAC)
PO Box 1335
Durant, OK 74702
Tel: (405) 924-5094 or (800) 658-2823

Science and Technology Research Center (STRC)
PO Box 12235
Research Triangle Park
Durham, NC 27709-2235
Tel: (919) 549-0671

NASA **Technology Transfer**
823 William Pitt Union
University of Pittsburgh
Pittsburgh, PA 15260
Tel: (412) 648-7000

Southern Technology Applications Center
Box 24
Progress Center, One Progress Boulevard
Alachua, FL 32615
Tel: (904) 462-3913; (800) 354-4832 (FL only);
(800) 225-0308

NASA/UK **Technology Applications Program**
University of Kentucky
109 Kinkead Hall
Lexington, KY 40506-0057
Tel: (606) 257-6322

Nerac, Inc.
One Technology Drive
Tolland, CT 06084
Tel: (860) 872-7000
www.nerac.com

Technology Application Center (TAC)
University of New Mexico
Albuquerque, NM 87131
Tel : (505) 277-3622

NASA **Industrial Application Center**
University of Southern California
Research Annex
3716 South Hope Street
Los Angeles, CA 90007-4344
Tel: (213) 743-6132; (800) 642-2872 (CA only);
(800) 872-7477

NASA/SU **Industrial Application Center**
Southern University
Department of Computer Science
Baton Rouge, LA 70813-9737
Tel: (225) 771-2060

5. Prototyping Contacts

Brown Venture Forum
William Jackson
Brown University, Box 1949
Providence, RI 02912
Tel: (401) 863-3528
Fax: (401) 863-1836
www.brownventureforum.org

Monthly meetings in which a selected topic and growing business is featured for analysis and discussion (forums begin in October and end in May). Start-up clinics in which early stage companies go before a panel of experts to receive constructive criticism and advice on their business plans. Educational workshops. Publications: *The Entrepreneur's Resource Guide* and *The Brown Venture Forum Newsletter.*

Small Business Administration (SBA)
409—3rd St., SW
Washington, DC 20416
Toll free: 1-800-U-ASK-SBA
www.sba.gov

(FREE) Entrepreneur guides for starting a business; computer and software for research; business plan development assistance; business counseling walk-in center; 24-hour Helpline call (800) 697-4636.

Small Business Development Center (RISBDC)
1150 Douglas Pike
Smithfield, RI 02917
Tel: (401) 232-6111
Fax: (401) 232-6933
www.risbdc.org

Provides broad-based and high-quality, no-cost consulting, and low-cost educational services.

Center for Design & Business

169 Weybosset Street, 2nd Floor
Providence, RI 02903
Tel: (401) 454-6108
Fax: (401) 454-6559
E-mail: info@centerdesignbusiness.org
www.centerdesignbusiness.org

Assists manufacturers and business owners in the utilization of design to develop more competitive products and businesses; provides guidance to businesses and individuals in the process of bringing new product designs and inventions to market; and provides business skills to artists and designers who are running businesses.

Business Development

Secretary of State Office, 100 North Main Street
Providence, RI 02903
Tel: (401) 222-2185
Fax: (401) 222-3890
E-mail: pcaranci@state.ri.us
www2.corps.state.ri.us/business_development/

Starting a business checklist; resource manuals and registration assistance; patents; trademarks; and the *Small Business Playbook*, a resource guide for small businesses.

Inventors' Digest®

30-31 Union Wharf
Boston, MA 02109
Tel: (617) 367-4540
Fax: (617) 723-6988
E-mail: inventorsd@aol.com
www.inventorsdigest.com

The official publication of the United Inventors Association of the USA and other inventor's associations.

Innovation Institute

852 Highway MM
Everton, MO 65646
Tel: (417) 836-5671
E-mail: questions@innovation-institute.com
www.innovation-institute.com

Inventor/innovator assistance service that provides an honest and objective analysis of the risks and potential of your idea, invention, or new product. They answer questions on invention evaluation, product assessment, international corporate participation, resources, and the World Innovation Network.

Management Roundtable

92 Crescent Street
Waltham, MA 02453
Tel: (800) 338-2223
Fax: (781) 398-1889
E-mail: info@roundtable.com
www.managementroundtable.com

Conferences, seminars, research, and publications on trends, technology, and best practices for speeding profitable products to market; publishes "Product Development Best Practices" report, and an interactive database of product development practices.

Product Development & Management Association (PDMA)

Bill Pawlucy
17000 Commerce Parkway, Suite C
Mount Laurel, NJ 08054
Tel: 1-800-232-5241
Fax: (856) 439-0525
E-mail: pdma@pdma.org
www.pdma.org

Helps improve the effectiveness of people engaged in developing and managing new products, both manufactured goods and services. Facilitates the generation of new information, and helps convert information into usable format. PDMA sponsors a yearly research competition and rewards up to three proposals with financial support and research access to PDMA members. It has a yearly conference and several regional ones. It publishes the *Journal of Product Innovation Management*, a newsletter, and *The PDMA Handbook of New Product Development*.

Slater Center for Design Innovation and Manufacturing

3 Davol Square,
Providence, RI 02903
Tel: (401) 831-6633
www.slaterdesmfg.com

Provides funding and mentoring to support the development of innovative businesses.

Invent Now

221 South Broadway Street
Akron, OH 44308
Tel: (330) 762-4463
E-mail: museum@invent.org
www.invent.org

A museum that also has an outreach program for inventors, a camp to teach kids creative skills, and an internship program. Also acts as a resource for inventors, has a store, and sponsors a competition for college students. Established by the US Patent & Trademark Office.

United Inventors Association of the USA

PO Box 23447
Rochester, NY 14692
Tel: (585) 359-9310
Fax: (585) 359-1132
E-mail: uiausa@aol.com
www.uiausa.org

A nonprofit, educational, and networking group; acts as a resource clearinghouse; provides online and telephone counseling. Provides support and services to inventors and inventor support groups; provides publications of interest, including a resource guide.

Wisconsin Innovation Service Center

University of Wisconsin-Whitewater
402 McCutchan Hall,
Whitewater, WI 53190
Tel: (262) 472-1365
Fax: (262) 472-1600
www.uww.edu/business/innovate/innovate.htm

Prepares new product feasibility research reports on market size, competitive intensity, existing patents, and demand trends. Also provides online workshops.

More great business titles from Self-Counsel Press!

Ask for these titles at bookstores and stationers or visit our website at *www.self-counsel.com*

Market Research Made Easy

Don Doman, Dell Dennison, and
Margaret Doman
$14.95
ISBN: 1-55180-409-3

- Learn how to analyze the market

- Increase your market share

- Measure the success of your marketing campaigns

Market research is not the exclusive territory of high-priced professionals. This book will show you how to do it yourself by asking the right questions and using existing information about your market, competition, and potential customers.

Low-Budget Online Marketing for Small Business

Holly Berkley
$14.95
ISBN: 1-55180-427-1

- Promote your company or product on the Internet

- Use the same tactics major corporations use

- Grow your business on a small-business budget

Large companies have huge budgets for marketing their products and services online. This book takes you behind the scenes of successful marketing campaigns. The book will show you how to cut costs so that you can adapt the same successful marketing strategies that big companies use for your business.

Getting Publicity

Tana Fletcher and Julia Rockler
$15.95
ISBN: 1-55180-312-7

- Get publicity for your organization

- Master the essential media skills for success

- Learn practical tools for low-cost exposure

Aimed specifically for organizations and individuals whose ambitions are bigger than the bankrolls, this book emphasizes low-cost, do-it-yourself promotional strategies. From newspaper articles to radio interviews, this expanded and updated edition includes all the advice you need to sparkle in the publicity spotlight.

Order Form

All prices are subject to change without notice. Books are available in book, department, and stationery stores. If you cannot buy the book through a store, please use this order form. (Please print.)

Name: _____

Address: _____

Charge to: ❏ Visa   ❏ MasterCard

Account number: _____

Validation date: _____

Expiry date: _____

Signature: _____

Yes, please send me:

_____ *Market Research Made Easy*

_____ *Low-Budget Online Marketing for Small Business*

_____ *Getting Publicity*

Please add $4.95 for postage and handling. Washington residents, please add 7.8% sales tax.

❏ Check here for a free catalog.

Please send your order to:

Self-Counsel Press Inc.
1704 North State Street
Bellingham, WA 98225